BEACH CHAIR DIARIES

Summer Tales from Maine to Maui

JANET E. SPURR

D0103641

FALMOUTH
HEIGHTS
BOOKS

Cover art by Forrest Rodts
www.forrestrodts.com
Back cover photo by Roger Farrington
www.rogerfarrington.com

Falmouth Heights Books
5 Bessom St. #208
Marblehead, MA 01945
Fax: 781-639-7725
www.beachchairdiaries.com
www.janetspurr.com

Library of Congress Cataloging-in-Publication Data

ISBN 978-0-9799850-4-1

Spurr, Janet
Beach chair diaries. Summer tales from maine to maui /
by Janet Spurr
p. cm.

Includes Bibliographical references and index.

1. Travel Essays

10 9 8 7 6 5 4 3 2

First Edition

This book is dedicated to:

My parents – who first brought me to the beach,

My brother – who taught me to love the beach,

My aunt – who loved the beach,

And most of all to God

– who created the beach.

Praise from other authors

"If you focus on fun, focus on the beach, and focus on the pages of *Beach Chair Diaries*, you'll find an endless summer of love and joy right in your own heart and soul."
—Jack Canfield, co-author of *Chicken Soup for the Soul* ®

"You can have summertime, anytime, simply by reading this book. The author's sunny nature shines through every page, and makes you feel like you're at your favorite shore's edge – even if it's 20 degrees outside. Janet Spurr's evocative writing shows her reverence for the water and reminds you of the magical effect of being in, on or around a lake, ocean or stream. Read it and reap."
—Sam Horn, author of *POP*, *Stand out in any crowd*, and *Tongue Fu*

"If you love summer and fun, then you will love *Beach Chair Diaries*. Janet's words will inspire you to buy a new bathing suit, get out your beach chair and head to the nearest shore."
—Wally Amos, author of *The Cookie Never Crumbles*, *Be Positive! Insights on How to Live an Inspiring and Joy-filled Life*

"While we are in a constant flight or fight mode, it is nice to daydream while Janet Spurr's stories take us swimming in laughter within the pages of *Beach Chair Diaries*."
—Malachy McCourt, author of *A Monk Swimming*, *Singing My Him Song*, and *Voices of Ireland*

"To know Janet is to love her and you'll know and love her after reading *Beach Chair Diaries*. Part memoir and part baby-boomer's guide to a less stressful life. Janet's breezy, inviting tone makes you want to find your own "beach," even if it's purely in your mind."
—Melanie Rigney, editor

"Janet Spurr is irrepressible and irresistible in her approach to life and words. In these pages, you'll discover her unparalleled spirit and spunk."
—Ronda Rich, author of *What Southern Women Know (That Every Woman Should)*

"Janet Spurr's *Beach Chair Diaries* is a total delight. You'll feel the breezes, hear the surf, and feel the sand between your toes."
—Thomas B. Sawyer – bestselling author of *No Place to Run*, former head writer of Murder, She Wrote

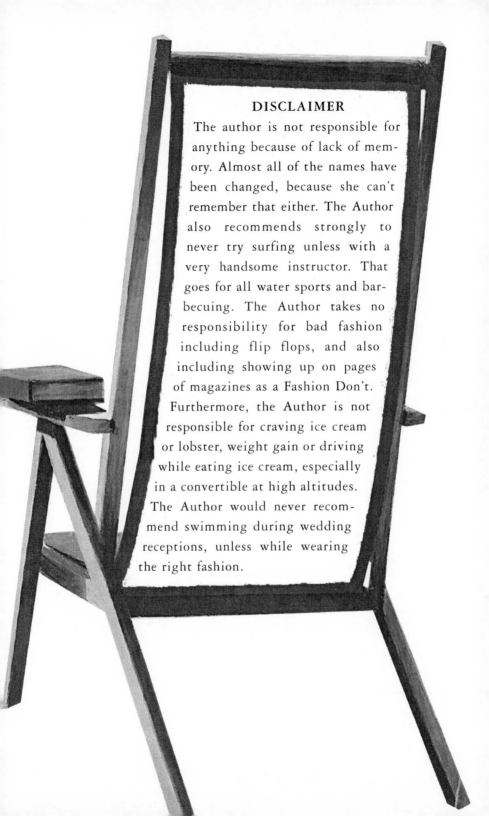

DISCLAIMER

The author is not responsible for anything because of lack of memory. Almost all of the names have been changed, because she can't remember that either. The Author also recommends strongly to never try surfing unless with a very handsome instructor. That goes for all water sports and barbecuing. The Author takes no responsibility for bad fashion including flip flops, and also including showing up on pages of magazines as a Fashion Don't. Furthermore, the Author is not responsible for craving ice cream or lobster, weight gain or driving while eating ice cream, especially in a convertible at high altitudes. The Author would never recommend swimming during wedding receptions, unless while wearing the right fashion.

CONTENTS

Waves Lapping at My Feet - 13

WATER SPORTS

Surfer Girl - 19

Boat in a Box - 29

Finding the Perfect Wave - 39

BEACH CHAIR APPRECIATION

Beach Chair Therapy - 47

In Search of the Perfect Beach Chair - 55

SUMMER FOOD

Why Not B.Y.O.L! - 65

Naked Ice Cream - 71

Do Lobsters Eat Real Men? - 77

CONVERTIBLE RIDES

Convertible Rides with Toilet Paper - 85

Can You Help Us Take Our Top Off? - 91

Convertible Ride to the Top of the World - 97

SUMMERTIME AGGRAVATIONS

Do Tourists Leave Their Brains at Home? - 105

How to Blow Up a Gas Grill - 111

Second Best Place to Get Water Out of Your Ear - 117

DRESSING FOR SUMMER

Flip-Flops - 123

Goodbye Lilly - 129

Swimming at Wedding Receptions - 135

BEACH WITHDRAWAL

A New England Dock - 145

That Summer Day - 149

Surfing Again - 155

Acknowledgements - 163

Author's Biography - 168

Waves Lapping at My Feet - an Introduction

One hot August day, I was sitting with my niece and sister-in-law on Wells Beach in Maine. Our chairs were stationed at the ocean's edge with the warm waves gently lapping over our feet. It was a picture-perfect day with little wind and some free time for relaxation. I turned to them and said, "I don't need a manicure or massage. I just need beach chair therapy."

I wrote Beach Chair Diaries so my readers could experience the simpler time of summer. Within these pages, you can ride along with me on the waves from Maine to Maui, eat lobster or ice cream from Boston to Belfast, Maine, and slowly walk along a beach in Nantucket on a hot August day. The beach is one of the few places left in the world that is stress free, where time seems to slow down. These days we all have insane schedules. Our lives have become enormously complicated as we constantly stare at clocks and computers.

At the beach, while free of distractions, I feel that I can finally relax. When I sit on my beach chair at the edge of the ocean, I realize how very simple it is: there's the sand, the water, the horizon; picking up a shell, a rock, or a piece of sea glass might be the only distraction.

Think about your favorite beach day. Sit back, close your eyes, and remember. Do you feel happier? More relaxed? Less stressed? Beach Chair Diaries will take you straight to the beach anytime. These pages are dedicated to fellow beach lovers who lust for it, miss it, and need to feel the beach throughout the year. During the 1960s, a movie called *Endless Summer* came out. It's about two surfers who follow summer around the world with their long boards, hunting waves and searching for the heat of the sun. My book will fuel an endless summer imagination.

Days at the beach have been a part of me since before I was born. My parents met while working on Cape Cod. After they were married and bought their first home, my father filled the basement with sand to host a beach party one January night. My mother told me there were sand flies in the house for weeks afterward, but the party was fantastic.

My first eight summers were spent on a Cape Cod beach. Falmouth Beach was two blocks from my grandparents' guest house. While I played in the waves, my brother, David, would dig big holes in the sand. When I came out of the water, he would throw me in a hole. I would yell and scream to get him to help me out. Now we spend August afternoons riding waves and screaming from boogie boards as we zoom into the shore. Although he is in his fifties and I'm fifty-something, we act as if we are nine years old.

While I was writing this book, I thought it would only be about summer fun and the inspiration of nature. However, a deeper message emerged: believe in your dreams and trust your passions. When I believed in my passion to write about summer, I found that my dream of being a writer came closer to reality, but the delays helped me learn too.

Without the help of a great many people, this book would not have made the beach as accessible to you. These people are not only outstanding in their careers and have a true passion for their work, but they live or work near the beach and love it. I was lucky enough to meet them while attending the Maui Writers Conference.

I still smile when I think that I met my mentor, Karen Horowitz, in Maui. Although she lives six blocks from me on Boston's North Shore, we had never met until we had hotel rooms in Maui next door to each other. I also met Melanie Rigney, a great editor for my book, in Maui; and a third person, Sam Horn, whose marketing expertise as my book coach taught me how to focus on the combination of writing and marketing, lived in Maui and now lives on the coast of Virginia. All these people understood my quest to be an author and helped me bring the inspiration of nature to you, believe in my dreams and trust my passion.

My biggest lesson was learning to ask for help. But more importantly, I learned to relax and remember to enjoy life's simple pleasures. It's a difficult balance, but with a beach chair peace of mind, it can be achieved.

To help you on your way, each essay in this book is followed by Low Tide Time, a time to recollect warm summer days. Step into some memories of your own.

Beach Chair Diaries is my gift to you. Please accept it, wrapped in sea grass. Now, go find a comfortable chair, whether it is a beach chair in Maui or an office chair in Manhattan. Quench your thirst with this reflection of a warmer time, a slower time, summertime. And you can take that to the beach.

WATER SPORTS

Surfer Girl

Boat in a Box

Finding the Perfect Wave

Surfer Girl

For forty years, whenever a Beach Boys song plays on the radio, I have sung along and dreamed of being a surfer. The biggest problem is that I live in northern Massachusetts, where the waves are warm enough to surf for about two minutes during August.

But when the sounds of a Beach Boys tune float through me, I picture a perfect summer day with medium-sized waves and the sea temperature like bathwater. I imagine surfers running into the waves, carrying their colorful boards. I dream of being one of them. Then, reality slaps me down like a tidal wave. In real life, I'm somewhat out of shape and short. I have about as much chance of becoming a lean, bronzed surfer girl as of being a Parisian runway model.

I love the sea and yearn for it. To make my yearning become real, I spent years ferreting away precious frequent-flyer miles. Finally, I got my trip to Maui. It was on the Maui shoreline that I first discovered the grandeur, power, and majesty of real waves. I stared in reverence before leaping into them, celebrating the achievement of a lifetime dream.

Later, a colorful sarong hiding my not-so-tanned-Eastern-seaboard legs, I stopped at Maui Tacos for lunch. I looked up from my bright new white flip-flops and into the warm brown eyes of a surfer boy. I soon learned his name was Mikela. Mikela had long golden-blond hair streaked by the sun, and the kind of deep tan that rewards people who live on the beach with effervescent youth. Sadly, he was about twenty-five years old and in much better shape than I.

In the parking lot with my food in hand, I noticed his van with about six surfboards stacked on the roof. In my friendly New England way, I asked him, "Do you collect those things, or do they grow up there?" In the true Aloha spirit, he laughed and offered me a free surf lesson.

Before I could accept, I thought about three possibilities: first, I could make a complete fool of myself learning to surf in front of this young Adonis; second, I could continue to relax on my beach chair and not fall off it nearly as much as I would certainly fall off a surfboard; and third, maybe with the help of frequent-flyer miles, I could come back after a year of getting in shape before I took a crack at surfing. So, I turned down his offer of a lesson. I passed on taking my dream in hand.

For a year, I analyzed why I hadn't gone surfing. It was not only a tug of war in my mind, but a tug of waves in my heart. Why didn't I go surfing that day? Was I getting too old and too relaxed in beach chair heaven to want to try something new? Would I ever get back to Maui? I might have given up a once-in-a-lifetime opportunity to learn to surf. That winter, I dug out my 1972 junior lifesaving book and watched surfing movies. I worked out with weights and no longer felt the bottom of my upper arms jiggling. I also took advantage of every single frequent-flyer mile offered to mankind, or, in this case, womankind.

The next summer, I was lucky enough to have a twice-in-a-lifetime experience and returned to Maui. The second night I was there, I ran into Mikela, who was now a manager for Maui Tacos. This time, I took him up on a free surf lesson.

Early the next morning, he met me in front of my hotel. Feeling very fashionable in a new two-piece blue bathing suit, I had an extra-large cup of Kona coffee in one hand and my beach bag filled with everything except surfing ability in the other.

As we drove across the island around the sugar-cane fields to the best surfing beaches, we bonded, discovering our shared love for the ocean and water sports. Mikela's warm Hawaiian style helped me relax, but I was filled with eagerness and strong coffee. I was so excited I bounced on my seat like a three-year-old.

We drove up to Ho'okipa Beach and looked out to see the elephant-sized waves. My first thought was to run inland as far as I could. Mikela explained that part of the surfing ritual was to watch the waves and make sure this was the best area to surf. For the next twenty minutes, he stood in front of his van and watched the waves.

Being a polite person from Boston, I wanted to rip the surfboard off the roof and get started. But I had learned the Aloha Spirit and slowed down to appreciate the power and beauty of the Pacific Ocean.

The waves were crowded with about twenty surfers; and about thirty spectators were on the cliffs above. At last, Mikela helped me carry the large yellow long board down to the beach. My heart was racing; my palms felt sticky on the waxed board. This board weighed more than my luggage, and considering that I pack like Mrs. Howell from Gilligan's Island, that's heavy.

Mikela took the surfboard from me and laid it down on the beach. He taught me how to get up on it and stand, as if I were in the water. He was so kind. I wished that he wasn't twenty-five years old. Now not only did I have a chance to make a fool out of myself in front of this handsome young man but also show the rest of the crowd my midlife thighs, all the while sporting fashionable short black rubber windsurfing booties.

As we paddled out about 300 feet, I realized that even a year of lifting hand weights hadn't given my arms the strength needed for this sport. I prayed as I paddled hard into the breakwater and held onto my board inside the crashing waves, wondering if I could end the day right there and call that surfing. I tried to pay no attention to the fact that Mikela's van was getting smaller, that there might be sharks below me, and that this board to which I was attached by a rubber leash was the size of my Subaru. I used what courage I had gained from twenty-five years of skiing black diamond trails to fight my fear. I kept telling myself that falling into water is much easier than tumbling down a snow-covered mountain lined with big, solid pine trees. And warmer, too.

I found the most difficult part was the timing: watching for the wave, sitting while straddling the too-wide-to-be-comfortable long board, sliding onto and turning the board, paddling like a Mississippi River boat, and then standing up. At this point, I thought being a Parisian runway model would have been a lot easier. Getting used to straddling a long board in these waves was like trying to ride a whale at Sea World.

In the first two hours, I tried about 110 times to stand or even catch a wave. Almost the entire Pacific Ocean had gone up my nose. Being videotaped by the laughing Midwesterners drinking Mai Tais on the cliffs above didn't increase my confidence either.

Of course, the many professional surfers soaring toward me on long boards that could bash my brains out didn't make me nervous at all. I suddenly saw the whole situation as similar to Boston traffic, and all I needed to do was push down on the gas pedal.

As the sun scorched my back, I finally realized that even if I didn't get up, at least I had tried surfing. I had made the effort. More than anything I wanted to try again, for deep down inside I would be completely disappointed if I didn't surf.

Suddenly, a tropical rain began. The rain was the same temperature as the warm water. After a few moments of sprinkling, a brilliantly hued rainbow came out, and the beauty of Maui's emerald green landscape, indigo sky, and sapphire ocean helped ease my anxiety. I took a deep breath. Nature was giving me a moment to rest and reach down deeper for strength. And I was praying that my arm muscles would stop hurting.

After further attempts to stand up on the board, I noticed that Mikela was growing tired too. He decided to help me by pushing on my board to gain speed into the wave.

Finally, my board caught a wave! The surfboard ascended and slid with the indigo water, speeding in competition with a white cresting wave. The wave surged below me. I made a wobbly effort to stand as the board rode the wave. My rubber booties grabbed the surf-wax layered onto the board, and this gave me stability. My arms were outstretched, or maybe I wished they looked that way. I felt as if I was flying. Standing vertical on top of a wave, soaring across the water, I had conquered the ocean! I was a surfer girl at last! I wanted all the surfers to stop in the middle of a wave to clap. Although it lasted just a nanosecond before I tumbled into the ocean, it will always be a Kodak moment.

After a dozen more unsuccessful attempts to ride the waves, we began wearily paddling toward shore. My hands were wrinkled as prunes. My whole body ached. No one could pay me enough to make me raise my arms over my head. My ponytail holder was now in the possession of some mermaid. My hair looked as if I had used wallpaper glue as mousse. I was so beat that the board carried me into the sharp coral. I didn't even notice that it nicked my leg and I was bleeding. Great, now I was shark bait. Like a sailor, I wanted to kneel and kiss the warm sand. I was totally exhausted but filled with a sweet contentment. I watched the waves I had conquered with a new attitude. I had done this. I had achieved my dream. I was a real live surfer girl.

LOW TIDE TIMES

Take a summer memory break.

Are you interested in catching your own wave, whether it is bodysurfing, windsurfing, water skiing, jet skiing, or boogie boarding?

Because of embarrassment or cellulite, do you analyze all the reasons why you couldn't try this sport and then give up? Never let age, flab, or dignity stop you. Go do it.

How about taking out your summer calendar to mark a day or two to relax or to try that sport?

Spurr's tips:
Try a sport that you've always wanted to do.

Find a course for it online.

www.surflifeforwomen.com Surf Life For Women Magazine, Morro Bay, CA

www.surfline.com Huntington Beach, CA

Boat in a Box

Iㅅ was hot on the North Shore of Boston a few summers ago, so I went to Sears to buy a fan. The parking lot melted my shoes with every step. I turned around to look for gooey footprints. It took half my strength to press open the heavy glass door. The chill of the store's air conditioning greeted me like a tidal wave. I took my first breath and thought perhaps I should just go to the bedding section and test a mattress.

Instead, I stumbled toward the whirring display of electric fans. A half-hour later, I walked out with a boat in a box. This was not just any vessel, but a four-person, blue-gray-striped Sevylor inflatable dinghy with oarlocks, tie-offs for dock lines, and the possibility of mobility with just one extra accessory—a wooden engine mount.

I felt this was a bargain at ninety dollars. I can still hear the sound of the cash register: Ka-ching! I was a boat owner! After fourteen summers of sailboat racing on other people's boats, I was so excited that the Concorde couldn't have flown me to the dock near my apartment quickly enough.

I had spent many seasons as part of a sailboat racing crew. We raced on forty-one-foot and forty-seven-foot boats. Although I was enthusiastic and learned spinnaker takedowns and other jobs, I was never taught to handle a boat single-handedly, but I had fun when we raced around New England or Antigua.

I had rented a small apartment in the back of a condo complex located on Marblehead Harbor, which was considered one of the quaintest harbors in New England. Although less than three miles long and half a mile wide, during the summer the harbor is filled with more than three hundred boats. About 75 percent of the boats are sailboats sporting masts that fill the summer sky.

The small dock next to my complex was always the best place to find my neighbors and, in this case, several pairs of lungs for a blow-up-the-boat party. As my neighbors—the Shelbys, the Reeds, and Dean Amato—took turns huffing and puffing, the first-prize neighbor, Dean, offered to lend me his 3.5-horsepower motor. I offered to wash his car for the rest of his life.

Two minutes later, I was on the phone ordering that essential wooden engine mount. For some reason, a little voice inside my head kept asking, "Why did you buy this boat?"

The next morning, the sun came up, and the FedEx man arrived. I was so excited to be closer to my life on the seas that the FedEx man could have been Prince William and I wouldn't have noticed. I practically grabbed the box, signed for it, and ran out the door, even before the FedEx man was back in his truck. I quickly discovered that an engine mount was an overpriced one-by-two-foot wooden board with four screws. The cost was ninety dollars. Ka-ching!

I was the proud owner of a blow-up boat, and I soon realized the truth of boat owners' laments, that any size boat is a hole in the water into which one throws money. Whether an owner spends two hours blowing up a boat or two months painting one, it's the same amount of aggravation. I suggest that boat ownership should be with a partner who might have an enormous trust fund and who also has recently lost his or her mind.

Another aspect of boat ownership is the challenge of purchasing the exact accessories. For instance, the oars manufactured for the Sevylor Inflatable looked like plastic Barbie-doll oars, so I decided to buy a larger wooden pair. They were big and wide and did not fit my boat's oarlocks. After yet another trip to the store to purchase the correct oars, I wanted to take the Barbie-doll-sized oars and beat the sales clerk over the head.

The next day was scheduled as Maiden Voyage Day. As I proudly carried the fully inflated boat from my apartment deck down to the dock, a strong northeast wind blew up from nowhere. Suddenly, I looked like the Flying Nun, but in place of a habit I was wearing my blow-up boat. I lashed the boat to the dock and returned to my apartment for the thirty-pound motor. My valiant friend Don arrived just in time to lug the motor down to the dock and try to attach it to the ninety-dollar mount on the aft end of the boat. Don and I had been sailing buddies, celebrating summer during many weekend parties with a great circle of friends.

Well, this was no party. We finally managed to attach the motor while bobbing up and down in my inflatable boat as the dock scratched our arms. Then we almost dropped the engine into the harbor. While trying to lift it, our arms were almost ripped out of their sockets. Finally, we lifted the engine and placed it on the wooden mount. At this point we didn't know whether to laugh or cry. But we laughed. Then we started pulling on the engine cord, the first of about a thousand pulls. Nothing worked, not even a thousand prayers. No engine sounds disturbed that early summer evening. All we could hear was the quiet breeze on the water and the clicking of halyards on aluminum masts.

Feeling frustrated and landlocked with my

dreams of cocktails at sunset on the open sea sunk, I thanked my valiant friend Don and dragged the motor over to Mobil Marine. Within a few minutes, they repaired it for ninety dollars. Ka-ching!

Perhaps what was most frustrating was that both my great-grandfathers had been sea captains— and my own knowledge of boats was limited to the one or two jobs I had when racing sailboats. I should have paid more attention instead of socializing with my fellow crew members.

Carrying the motor to and from the dock was making my arms as big as both my great-grandfathers' arms combined. This weightlifting was also causing me to outgrow my shirts, so I needed a new nautical wardrobe. Besides, those horrid orange life preservers I had just purchased clashed with everything, especially the four-person, blue-gray-striped inflatable. This was a great excuse for buying new boat shoes and nautical wear to match. Ka-ching!

After the engine had been repaired and attached to my boat, Kelly and Dee arrived. Kelly and I had been friends for more than thirty years and worked together while I was in high school. I had introduced Kelly to her husband, and she convinced me to move to Marblehead. I first met Dee when I moved to Marblehead. A buyer for a clothing company, she became a business client and a friend in the same week.

They ran down to the dock with a bottle of champagne, fresh enthusiasm, and the perfect name for my Sears and Roebuck purchase: *Rowbuck,* spelled *Row$*. Champagne in hand, I stood with Kelly, Dee, and the neighbors on the dock, ready for the inaugural launch.

My neighbors—the Shelbys, the Reeds, Dean, and Perry—gathered for the big moment. Perry was the character of the condo complex, always armed with a good joke and sporting a starched shirt. The Shelbys and Reeds were rollicking couples who had more fun boating, dining, and laughing than most twenty-year-olds I know. I first met Dean when he offered me a free lobster and later found out we were born less than two weeks apart.

I had imagined my inaugural launch with everyone standing around holding lighted candles and bottles of champagne to christen my boat, but since it was an inflatable, that wasn't going to happen. Then someone mentioned fuel. Ka-ching! I thanked God that the fuel, unlike everything else, didn't cost ninety dollars. Was there no end to the amount of money needed to enjoy a nice harbor cruise? At this point, had I been in the Navy, I probably would have gone AWOL.

When the crew finally pushed off the old gray wooden dock, I pulled on the engine cord. The engine had too much power. Consequently, we sputtered around and around in circles until I lowered the throttle, which in turn made the motor die. Over and over, this scenario repeated itself, without enough time between engine starts and stops to have a glass of champagne. Dee managed to sip half of a glass before it spilled all over her.

Another problem was that the four-person boat was not meant to accommodate four adults. It would have been more suitable for one adult and three small circus animals. The weight of the three of us submerged the boat halfway in the water.

As we went around in circles, Kelly and Dee tried to enjoy themselves while holding on for dear life. I began to see that boat ownership wasn't for me. I had been good at my sales job for over two decades. I also could throw a dinner party for fourteen at the drop of an ice cube, with several friends to help. At this point I knew I needed help. I also realized that my two good friends' lives were in my hands as we dodged the bigger boats coming toward us in the crowded harbor, so I steered us closer to shore. My half-sunk boat filled with three women must have looked like a refugee vessel from Cuba.

Kelly kept saying, "Thank God my husband doesn't know I'm here."

Eventually, after traveling across the harbor, *Row$* found the rocks and the harbor tour ended with the four-person, blue-gray inflatable tied up against the starboard side of a yacht-club tender.

When we reached land, Dee kissed the dock. Kelly drank the champagne, and I explained to my neighbors how the rocks across the harbor had jumped up out of nowhere. The rotor-chipped engine made a return engagement to Mobil Marine. Ka-ching!

Of the six neighbors remaining on the dock, only Perry could choke back enough laughter to speak. He smiled, put an arm around me, and said, "Well, Spurr, Row$ will make a nice inflatable planter in the fall."

Weeks later, I sat on the dock watching the boats float by while I read and wrote and was content. My life was quieter. I was no longer caught up in boat maintenance. Instead, I was caught up in relaxation and writing. Nothing had turned out perfectly with Row$, but I'm glad I tried it. The best parts were that I didn't spend thousands of dollars, and that nobody got hurt, other than my ego. I tried to look at the positive side of being landlocked. I would write more and relax more. Even though boat ownership didn't work for me, I had learned to ask for help, and that was big for me.

Now when anyone says, "Oh, you live in Marblehead, you must own a boat," I start laughing and reply, "I once had a boat . . . "

LOW TIDE TIMES

Did you have a summer vacation day that didn't go as planned? Perhaps it rained, and so you read a great book, took a nap, and relaxed for the entire day.

How about a time when something went wrong and caused a mechanical disaster, but it turned into a funny situation?

Think about that day, laugh, and breathe.

<u>Spurr's tips:</u>

Use other people's boats.

Charter a boat.

Finding the Perfect Wave

As the wave retreats, I check to see if my bathing suit is still on. I may feel like a child, but I'm not.

At South Beach on Martha's Vineyard, I leave striped umbrellas, radios, and dunes covered with beach roses and race into the sea. Back on shore, waves crash endlessly near my wet, sand-caked feet. I listen to the surf and watch the shells as they withdraw into the sea. Salt water runs through my soul after so many summers of bodysurfing on Cape Cod.

The waves capture me now. I seize the wave that rushes, breaks, crashes, and glides me into a white-foamed, salty sea. I twist and tumble to shore after being dragged onto the sand. I look back, laughing, wanting to capture another. I dive back, my arms slicing the water like swords. Saltwater slicks back my hair and warmly wraps around my waist. I wait to capture the crest.

The beach sounds end after I dive in. The quiet underwater world encircles me. The salty bubbles follow me up to the surface as I watch and wait for the white crest to build.

When I turn back to shore, a wave knocks me off balance. Salt water invades me, stinging the inside of my nose. Small strings of green seaweed float near me. The warm winds caress my face. The cloudless blue July sky stretches summer around me. I push off the sandy floor and dive, dolphin like, once again into the silence below.

As I surface, a huge wave starts to crest two feet in front of me. I hold my breath and swim to it. My feet kick hard for speed, with my arms outstretched just as it breaks. Holding on, I slide with the wave and the power of the sea, surfing all the way to shore until the sand greets my stomach.

In total freedom, I surf the waves to find that perfect one. As each surges, it holds a new mystery for me. I dive into the waves quickly, but cautiously. The powerful ocean plays with me as I gamble with it. The hours pass slowly, almost stopping summertime. I step out of the waves to ground myself in the sand and then return to the sea and bodysurf in the waves' clutches.

Later, when I join my friends, we compare how much sand we've collected inside our bathing suits, piling up the sand to see who has the most at the end of the day.

Near sunset, my body is sticky and salt-crusted. One tumble has left a red scrape on my left thigh. In the distance, a lifeguard blows his piercing whistle, and the swimmers scream at the next big wave. As my toes grab the sand once more, I am nine years old again.

LOW TIDE TIMES

When was the last time you played in the waves at the ocean or in a water park?

Do you love or fear the water?

Have you ever had sand in your bathing suit? Was it a pain in the butt, or did you wear it as a badge of honor?

Have you ever stopped during a summer day to feel the slowness of summer? What happened?

Have you listened to waves and heard the shells or stones retreating into the sea?

Spurr's tips:
Buy Coastal Living magazine.

Go to a water park.

See if the library has a CD of ocean sounds.

BEACH CHAIR APPRECIATION

Beach Chair Therapy

In Search of the Perfect Beach Chair

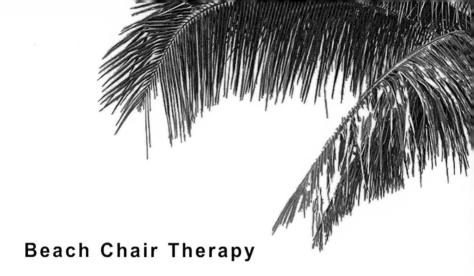

Beach Chair Therapy

I was probably conceived on a beach. My parents met at Falmouth Heights Beach in the summer of 1938 while working at the Terrace Gables Hotel. Born in January, I imagine I was sitting on a beach by the time I was six months old, if not sooner. My grandparents had a guesthouse two blocks from the beach. Ocean water is part of my family's blood.

Recently, I put my family's movies on video. On a cold rainy day, I watched the old footage of a past beach vacation when my older brother dug big holes in the sand and threw me in.

My brother, David, is over fifty now and he and his family hit the beach every summer like Normandy soldiers. They establish a beachhead by 10 a.m. and do not surrender until the sun goes down. From their quaint clapboard cottage, which is just two blocks from the water, they drag five boogie boards, four inner tubes, three coolers stuffed with food, colorful plastic pails with shovels, several beach towels, sweatshirts, five gallons of suntan lotion, beach chairs for everyone, and a partridge in a pear tree. The only calamity they are not prepared for, other than a nuclear holocaust, is rain. And all this is intended for a family of four.

Depending on my summer work schedule, I usually visit their Cape Cod rental cottage for a day or two. At the beach I watch David, decked out in his windsurfing booties, wrap-around sunglasses, and a white plastic safari hat. On his enlarged black inner tube, he floats off toward the sea wall, waiting for the waves. Although he is my older brother, sometimes I feel that I'm the adult.

On top of the tube, he leans back and lets the waves pound him toward the seawall. When his feet hit the wall, he pushes off, bouncing back out to sea. This continues for hours, even though the water can be a mere sixty-five degrees. David and his good friend, Ward, continue the ritual for the entire day. My brother's family, Ward's family, and I watch them, waiting for one of their inner tubes to be punctured by a sharp rock and send them soaring into the air.

On one cool June afternoon, I left the beach at

4 p.m. for a hot shower before an early dinner. With so many people staying at the cottage, I took advantage of the outside shower. One of the greatest experiences of summer is using an outdoor shower and staring up into the open sky.

Afterward, inside the cottage, I heard my thirteen-year-old niece say, "He's still down at the beach. If he doesn't come up soon, we're going to be late for dinner."

I looked at my mellow sister-in-law and pointed at my niece. "When did she become an adult?"

When I went outside, David and Ward were dragging their extra-large inner tubes toward their cottages. Covered with sand and salt and still wearing their sunglasses and hats, they were grinning from ear to ear. They had experienced their freedom of summertime.

A few summers later, my brother rented a cottage at Wells Beach, Maine. The beach is the size of several football fields but has no seawall, so David traded the inner tube for a boogie board. He also traded the warmer temperatures of Cape Cod's water for that of Maine's water—an insane sixty degrees, even in August.

The waves and my lack of time off called me to Wells Beach to join my brother and his family. One morning I ran along the beach. As I jogged by other runners and walkers, I noticed people sitting in chairs at the edge of the water. Already parked there at 9 a.m., they would be there for hours, only moving back their chairs as the tide came in.

I smiled and thought, "That's exactly what I need to do. Sit with the waves lapping at my feet." As usual, my brother and his family arrived on the scene, outfitted with the entire stock of beach equipment from aisle four of Wal-Mart.

I pointed toward the people sitting at the edge of the water and said, "Look, serious beach chair people."

My sister-in-law smiled and immediately moved all the beach chairs closer to the waves. This was no small task, considering the width of the beach and the amount of stuff they had brought. That summer my brother finally purchased a small inflatable raft to haul all their beach equipment. He would drive his car two blocks from the cottage to the beach and then drag the raft the rest of the way, filled with enough paraphernalia to start a YMCA camp.

As we sat there, the waves gently lapped over our feet. I turned to my sister-in-law and niece and said, "Who needs a manicure, a massage, or a therapist? I just need beach chair therapy!"

We let the waves roll over our feet until the tide came in, eventually crashing and almost knocking us into the water. We laughed as our chairs nearly fell over. In front of us, we watched as my brother and his thirteen-year-old son, Andrew, rode the waves for hours on their boogie boards. Finally at 5 p.m., they folded up the chairs and packed everything to head for the cottage, but the waves still called to us. I looked at my brother, who was ready to drag the raft to the car. "David, look at the waves."

He turned, looked, and said, "You want to go back in?"

His family wasn't surprised. We grabbed the boogie boards and raced down the long beach. It was as if we hadn't caught a wave all summer. Our excitement overcame our craziness for venturing into sixty-degree water again. As a New Englander in August, I know there aren't many warm sunny days left, so no matter what the temperature of the water might be, I must do what I must do.

We waited for the waves, rode the waves, fell off the boards, and soared toward the shore. We laughed in the hot August sun and let our feet go numb. A forever bond floated between us. David stood waiting for the next wave, wearing his wrap-around sunglasses. He wore ridiculously loud red surf shorts with large black-and-white hibiscus flowers, unaware that the white pockets hung outside them.

He called, "Ja, look at the third wave." We turned, jumped on the boards, and caught it. Our legs vibrated with the force of the sea, sending us riding and screaming side-by-side into the shallow water. He steered into my board and we crashed at the edge of the water. Then we laughed and laughed. Our laughter was as loud as the pounding surf. People strolled by, wondering why adult-sized people were acting and sounding like five-year-olds. That day, we caught summer forever, my brother David and I. It was the perfect ride.

LOW TIDE TIMES

When was the last time you went to a beach, lake, or pool?

Where was the last place you went on vacation?

While on vacation, was there an hour when you did nothing?

Do you feel guilty when you do nothing?

When did you last sit and dangle your toes in the water?

Spurr's tips:
Next time you are at the beach, put your beach chair down next to the water.

Time yourself and see if you can do nothing for an hour.

In Search of the Perfect Beach Chair

My idea of making a major decision while on vacation is thinking about what is the best position for my beach chair. Should it be upright for writing or reading, midway for relaxing, or all the way down flat for serious tanning or snoozing?

Several years ago, I hung a brochure for the Maui Writers Conference on my bedroom wall. On the cover was a photo of a three-hundred-yard fountain in front of the Grand Wailea Resort, flowing past the palm trees into the Pacific. No matter how many people tried to explain the beauty of Hawaii—Don Ho could have sung to me in my living room—I still couldn't have visualized it. I'm convinced God did not rest on the seventh day; He made Hawaii. And at last, I was on my way.

When I stepped off the plane, I was surprised that no one presented me with a lei. I noticed that a few newlyweds were getting leis. When the shuttle-bus driver found me, I thought he was hiding a lei behind his back. Unfortunately, he wasn't. I wanted my lei.

As we drove across a lush, tropical landscape, the warm Hawaiian winds swayed the palm trees. My heart pounded when we approached the lights of the Grand Wailea Resort. As we continued up the long driveway, I was so excited to be there that my hands were sweating. I opened the door of the shuttle bus, and in front of me stood a perfectly beautiful woman who presented me with a fuchsia lei and said, "Aloha." I was as thrilled about having these orchids around my neck as I would be kissing a Calvin Klein underwear model. But that's another beach chair story. Instead, I kissed her on both cheeks.

The bellman rolled my luggage through the main entrance and passed the fountains, which were surrounded by flowers, and he offered me a choice of guava punch or ice water. He disappeared for a moment and returned with a glass of pink guava punch on a silver tray.

I sipped the drink, turned to another beautiful Hawaiian woman behind the front desk, and said, "I think I'm going to like it here."

I took note of the hotel lighting, a golden relaxing color. Of course, after fifteen hours of traveling, anything might appear relaxing. Had there been a mattress in the lobby, I would have slept on it.

When I arrived in my room, I wanted to change my mailing address to Room #4208. The only thing missing was Romeo below the balcony. The bathroom was almost as big as my entire apartment. I could have hosted a dinner party next to the sink.

After the bellman left, I changed into shorts and ran down to the ocean, sticking my feet into the warm Pacific for the first time in my life. The night sounds of paradise surrounded me with the chirping of the frogs and palm fronds moving in the wind. I inhaled the scent of the plumeria trees. After wandering around the marble stairs, the fountains, pools, slides, and waterfalls, I searched for a perfect beach chair, but instead I found the chapel.

I entered and fell to my knees in silence. The words "Thank You" just didn't seem to express enough gratitude. Friends would have paid to see that Maui made me speechless.

I love arriving at a new destination at night and awakening the next morning to find a whole new treasure. Still on Boston time, I awoke at 5:30 a.m. I am not a morning person, but when I slid open the wooden balcony doors, felt the winds, and saw the green palm trees, I knew I had to conquer the Pacific waves and find that perfect beach chair.

That morning, I walked around the pools,

whirlpools, and fountains in search of that chair. I thought it might be by the largest pool, the Activity Pool. I was so excited I tried one chair after another, moving closer and closer to the pool. When I stopped moving, I asked a Japanese woman to take a picture of me on the beach chair, with its flag up to signal the waitress. After a while, I somehow knew there was a better beach chair. Finding it was a quest similar to my whole life, always looking for a better job, a better apartment, or a better place to vacation.

I walked up the stairs, past the white plumeria trees, and found paradise: the Hibiscus Pool. At the end of the famous fountain I recognized from the brochure picture that had graced my bedroom wall years before, there was a huge half-circle pool with a fountain cascading down into it. This pool is for adults only; all one hears is the water from the fountain and waitresses offering frozen drinks or plastic surgery.

The pool had several wide steps down into it; most people sat on these steps or floated on a raft and read. Most important for me, the Hibiscus Pool had the Perfect Beach Chair: crafted from teak, the chair was a step away from the pool and had padding as thick as my mattress. A soft blue cotton cover and cushion prevented unwanted sliding—or sticking. And positioning? This perfect beach chair reclined to any position, including my favorite one, called

"George Clooney, Take Me!" Some of the beach chairs needed to be moved with the sun. No problem; the staff were part-time weightlifters. Some of the beach chairs had teak tables attached. When one of my chairs didn't have a table, I asked the pool staff to bring me one. It was then that I thought, "I have become a princess."

On my second day at the pool, one staff person had a tray of white rolled towels. I was almost afraid to ask. "What are those?"

He smiled, offering the tray. "Ice-cold towels. Would you like one?"

I laughed. "You have got to be kidding. I have to take a picture of this."

While I relaxed on this padded piece of paradise and the Hawaiian winds touched my soul, I wrote. But sometimes I would fall asleep after having shrimp salad and a Perrier.

With the Pacific Ocean about three hundred yards away, the sound of the crashing waves could compete with the percussion in a Beethoven symphony. Every hour I would step into the whirlpool; swim slowly across the quiet pool; walk down the stairs, passing what seemed like steerage-class; use the slides; take a swim in the Pacific; and then return to the Perfect Beach Chair. Strolling up to the chair was a promenade back to paradise. The manicured green lawns, pink hibiscus, palm trees, and weddings taking place at the nearby chapel all made it seem like a fantasy.

I've been lucky enough to return to Maui a few times to rediscover paradise and to experience it in different ways. During one trip in December, the Hibiscus Pool was closed for renovation, so I chose a beach chair and moved it to the edge of the Pacific. I can still hear the palm trees swaying, see the emerald mountains in the background, and feel the waves breaking on my feet.

Finding paradise makes life easier. It doesn't bother me that Maui is twelve hours away from home. Paradise could be on Mars, and my soul would still be content to have found it. I count the days until I return, which I pray is every year. Maybe it's not the beach chair, but the moment and the memories. My current computer screensaver has a picture of me sitting on this beach chair; Perrier never has tasted the same.

As my Aunt Bits says, "I'm investing in my memories."

Thank you, God, and thank you, American Express.

LOW TIDE TIMES

Have you ever taken a trip you have always dreamed about? Where?

If you haven't taken that trip, why not?

Do you feel you deserve it? Why or why not?

What is your idea of paradise?

Why not collect pictures of this paradise and hang them up?

<u>Spurr's tips:</u>
www.grandwailea.com

www.visitmaui.com

SUMMER FOOD

Why not B.Y.O.L?

Naked Ice Cream

Do Lobsters Eat Real Men?

Why Not B.Y.O.L?

Problem: Your wallet is thinner than it was in the eighties, but your tastes are just as expensive. You're in the mood for a lobster. What to do?

Solution: Boil water, buy corn, plan a dinner party, call your guests, and tell them, B.Y.O.L! Bring Your Own Lobster.

When I first moved to the North Shore of Boston, I relaxed on the dock of my condo complex. I sat in my lime-green beach chair on a hot summer day, checking out the sailors on the next dock.

A neighbor, Dean, came up to me, put his hand gently on my shoulder, and asked, "Would you like a hot dog, a hamburger, or lobster?"

I replied, "Is this a trick question?"

Since that summer day, I have become steeped

in the lore of lobster. On the North Shore it's difficult to go two blocks, let alone two towns, without seeing a supermarket or fish market that sells lobster. There also are many unusual spots to buy lobster-to-go. One such place is at the end of Marblehead Harbor. Paul has been selling lobster from the same spot for more than twenty years. He's there every weekend from May until October. He stands at the top of a set of steps that are next to the harbor where his lobster traps are set. He wears high rubber boots and has a scale swinging in the breeze.

On a sunny July day, I drove up to his spot, rolled down my window, and laughingly asked, "Medium coffee and a Honeydew doughnut?"

He leaned over. "Do you want cream and sugar with that?"

I parked my car, got out, and picked up a few lobsters to go.

At the Marblehead Lobster Company, a store a little farther up the coast, I asked Scott for a funny lobster story. He told me that people come in, look at the lobsters swimming in the water tanks, and ask, "Are those lobsters fresh?"

I knew a waitress in Maine who told all the tourists, "You can eat any part of the lobster except the left claw." At the end of the night, she and the staff would sit back and feast on buckets of left claws.

I have always wondered who was the first brave,

hungry soul who attempted to eat lobster. I'm told that at one time lobsters crawled around on the beaches and were so plentiful that they were picked up to feed the servants.

I found the word lobster in the dictionary. It was located between lobotomy and local government. Of the three, which is the most appealing?

Getting back to the B.Y.O.L. party, here are a few suggestions to make it a fun evening:

1. Tell your guests to bring small lobsters, the same size, so there is no mix up. If you have Martha Stewart tendencies, embroider monogrammed wristbands for the lobsters.

2. Ask each guest to bring a salad, a potato, or some corn on the cob. Provide the appetizers and desserts (in case anyone's still hungry), and boil water for the lobster and corn. Borrow a lobster pot or buy a big stainless steel pot at a discount store.

3. Invite one assassin or hit man to drop the lobsters into the boiling water, so you can see those crustaceans jerk around.

4. Make sure your guests are armed with the appropriate lobster utensils: crackers and pokers are available for a dollar or two in most stores, or

guests can share. Sometimes I use a hammer or rock to crack the shells. I always carry my lobster rock with me in case of a lobster-dining emergency.

5. For more advanced connoisseurs, rent a video of Annie Hall to brush up on some of the finer points of racing games for your lobsters.

The evening after my first B.Y.O.L party, my neighbor Dean invited me over for lobster. When I arrived, I confessed to the group that I had had lobster the night before. Dean asked if he could borrow extra lobster crackers to break open the claws. After watching the steam seeping out from the tail of my boiled supper and seeing that tantalizing dish of melted butter, I took out my emergency rock. I suddenly couldn't wait any longer to eat lobster again. I told Dean to get a hammer, and we all cracked away.

LOW TIDE TIMES

When was the last time you had friends over for a potluck dinner? Why not plan it now?

Are you nervous about hosting a dinner party?

Have you had lobster or one of your favorite meals with friends in the last year?

Do you know that lobster can be shipped anywhere in the world?

If you don't like lobster, would you consider cooking shrimp?

Spurr's tips:
Go to Legal Seafood's to find the freshest seafood
www.legalseafoods.com

Naked Ice Cream

Last night, I ate an entire pint of ice cream. Some people might consider this behavior a sign of depression. For me, it's utter ecstasy.

My parents started this ice cream obsession. One of my first memories is of my dad pretending to find a box of Eskimo Pies inside an ice-cube machine in the back of our favorite variety store. No one else in my family remembers this, but it's as vivid to me as any brightly colored pint of Ben and Jerry's. There are other childhood ice cream memories. During an extravagant European tour, my mother scheduled us to have ice cream at a German castle high above the Rhine. As our family strolled through the castle, I'll never forget the walls covered with antique tapestries. I felt very special as the staff greeted us and then served a dish of ice cream, European style, with a crisp cookie.

My love of ice cream continued and grew after college. In the fall after my graduation, a college friend and I moved to an apartment outside Boston. We were surprised to find that two other college friends, Heather and Cutler, had moved around the corner. Cutler was known for having the wildest parties in our dorm. Her first name was Barb, but no one ever called her that.

Cutler and I quickly discovered our common love for ice cream and the famous Steve's Ice Cream in Somerville, about a fifteen-minute drive from our apartments. Throughout the year, lines of people stretched outside the door and sometimes around the corner. Steve's was the first place I knew to serve "mix-ins"—candy, nuts, or fruit stirred into the freshly made ice cream. Almost as quickly as we found Steve's Ice Cream, we became best friends with all the employees. We even considered working there part-time. Of course, no partying had occurred while traveling to and from Steve's.

So off Cutler and I would go, every night, to Steve's. Eventually, we'd call ahead, find out the flavors, order a takeout, and pick it up while a hundred people or so stood in line. I usually ate my ice cream naked: no mix-ins, no sauce, nothing but ice cream.

During the blizzard of 1978, cars weren't

allowed on the road unless someone had an emergency. We considered three days without Steve's an emergency. We slowly drove through the streets piled ten feet high with snow on either side. We drove past the National Guard and through the middle of Harvard Square. We concocted a story about having to bring groceries to our grandmother, though of course we had no groceries. Luckily, we weren't stopped.

When we got to Steve's, the line was almost out the door. Everyone was sick of being stuck at home and had walked there. We ordered two pints: one for there and one to go. But this drive called for mix-ins. I ordered my usual coffee ice cream mixed with cookie dough ice cream, and added six spoons of Reese's Peanut Butter Cups, four spoons of Heath Bars, M&Ms, and chocolate chips, plus two whole Hershey Bars broken in long pieces. It was a snowstorm of mix-ins. Luckily, Cutler and I were very slender. Often we skipped our usual meals and made ice cream our dinner. During these many trips to Steve's, Cutler taught me how to reach over to shift the gears as she put in the clutch, held the steering wheel, and ate her ice cream.

Twenty years later, three college friends and I visited Cutler at her home in Washington, D.C. She is now known as Barb and has a nine-year-old son, whom she named Cutler. Her old roommate, Heather, and I flew in from Boston. Kathy, another dorm buddy, arrived from New York City, and Barb's old college roommate, Anne, flew in from Miami.

Barb had rented a hot tub in her backyard. Within an hour of our arrival, we raided her freezer to find more pints of ice cream than at a local grocery store. We each grabbed spoons and ate all the ice cream while lazing in the hot tub. We were no longer as thin as we had been in those days in Boston, but we were just as happy.

After Steve's was sold, the new owner's ice cream never was as good, so my search for the equivalent goes on throughout the land.

Once, while traveling on business down Route 1 in Belfast, Maine, I took a right turn on Route 3 to avoid the summer traffic and thought, "Isn't there an ice cream place down here on the left?" About two miles later, there it was. I realized then that I had been on the road in sales for too long, because I knew almost every place to find ice cream in New England.

Within two blocks of my house, an ice cream shop sells my new favorite treat, Mint Patty Frozen Yogurt. If I ate ice cream instead of frozen yogurt every day, I wouldn't be able to fit into my car. Mint Patty has miniature York Peppermint Patties in mint frozen yogurt. I can make the trip down and back to my house in three minutes.

One summer at a writers' workshop, one writer said he thought the greatest invention was the printing press. For me it was ice cream.

Another special ice cream place for me is a bit farther away. Last summer on Maui, I discovered Kona coffee ice cream and ordered it every other day, eating it while sitting in my perfect beach chair steps away from the Pacific. One afternoon, while my favorite waitress was serving a couple in the beach chairs behind me, she turned and asked me, "Isn't it about time for your ice cream?"

I turned to her and said, "I love you."

She brought me the Kona coffee ice cream. I held the cool plastic dish in my hand, stood up, and walked into the Jacuzzi. The warm water bubbled around me, the tropical winds blew through my hair, and I slowly ate the ice cream. If only Cutler were here.

LOW TIDE TIMES

When was the last time you bought ice cream?
Did you stop to sit and eat it and savor the taste?

Do you enjoy a unique food with a special friend?

When was the last time you were with that friend
to gorge on that food?

Could you talk on the phone with that person
while munching on this tasty treat?

Have you ever had this favorite food while in an
unusual place like a Jacuzzi or somewhere else?

Spurr's tips:
Go eat your favorite ice cream.

Do Lobsters Eat Real Men?

On vacation in Maine, I think it's almost the law to eat that famous red crustacean. Boiled lobster is so cheap that I feel I'm making money when I buy it. When the lobster is straight out of the freezing water, the taste is so fresh it seems as if it could slap me. But it can do more. After being assaulted by two lobsters, one man wound up in an ambulance. I'll tell that story later.

By my calculations, Maine takeout lobster spots outnumber McDonald's ten to one. Some restaurants even have red claws shaped into arches. Lobster restaurants can consist of anything from a trailer set up beside a river to outside picnic tables on the beach. Given the low cost of lobster, the comfort of a restaurant with an ocean view makes lobster therapy yet another obsession of mine.

During the summer of 2000, the outdoor lobster place closest to my brother David's cottage was closed due to lack of summer help. After ending a Beach Chair Therapy Day, my brother, his family, and I drove south on Route 1 in search of a new lobster spot.

The Lobsterman had a familiar red-and-white hand-painted sign. In back of it was a second sign, a flashing neon one that read: Plumbing and Heating.

After waiting for the August traffic jam to ease, I turned my car into the driveway, already smelling the lobster waiting to be dipped in melted butter. On the left were four large stainless-steel lobster pots steaming on top of propane tanks. A college kid held silver tongs over one uncovered pot. The steam covered his face and most of the entire yard.

I stopped my green Subaru beside him and asked. "Is this a drive-through lobster?"

He looked confused and already bothered by the many stupid questions of summer tourists. He snapped, "No."

"Then I'll have two Big Macs."

The cook laughed as I drove my car into the crowded parking lot.

When we got out of the car, David said, "This is great. Lobster, plumbing, heating. Plant a garden, and you'd never have to leave."

Inside The Lobsterman office were two small

tanks filled with swimming lobsters, a one-by-two-foot counter, and a pad of eight-by-ten-inch white lined paper. Sheets of paper from the pad were folded and torn into four equal sections. Each was inscribed with an order number, in green marker. We were number nine. Postcards from all over the world covered the walls. I could not find Marblehead or Maui, so I sent The Lobsterman cards from those places later that summer.

We noticed a laminated article from a Boston newspaper. Here is what I remember of the story: A man ventured into a supermarket to steal lobsters. He hid them in his pockets and left the store. The lobsters, unhappy in their new home, grabbed the man's attention below the belt. His screaming alerted workers, who found the man in the alley, bent over in excruciating pain. An ambulance and the police were called. The policeman was asked if the store would press charges.

The officer answered, "No, I think this man has been through enough already."

My brother and I went outside to wait for our number to be called. Soon, we gathered up three two-pound lobsters along with steamed clams and dessert. I paid twenty-nine dollars. I felt I was making money!

LOW TIDE TIMES

When did you last eat lobster or another special food?

Have you had dinner with your sibling without your parents or in-laws?

Why is it difficult not to include everyone?

When was the last time you invited your brother or sister for dinner and picked up the tab?

Could you plan this right now?

<u>Spurr's tips:</u>
Go to Maine and have lobster.

CONVERTIBLE RIDES

Convertible Rides with Toilet Paper

Can You Help Us Take Our Top Off

Convertible Rides to the Top of the World

Convertible Rides with Toilet Paper

Kate stabbed her four-inch heel into my foot and danced away in the yacht club ballroom. I held my foot as my dance partner held me. She had done it on purpose because of my fifteen-year friendship with Jack. I don't know if I was more shocked from the pain or the fact that my lawyer buddy Jack had chosen Kate for his new girlfriend. When she didn't drink, Kate was a genius of a lawyer and eventually would help Jack win his largest settlement of $3.3 million, but I wasn't crazy about her. Jack dated her on and off for a few years and had helped put her through law school.

As a boyfriend, Jack wasn't exactly a prize either. Sometimes he would try to bribe a girl to leave their relationship. One smart brain cell of mine decided years ago that I would do much better with Jack as a friend than as a boyfriend.

One August, during a regatta in Marblehead, Jack had rented a room at the Pleasant Inn. Staying aboard a forty-one-foot sailboat with ten crew members was about as comfortable as dancing beside Kate. On Saturday night of that regatta weekend, Kate became upset when Jack spent most of the evening talking to a girl named Vicki. Kate wanted to leave and drive back to Boston. Even though I disliked this foot-stomping woman, I tried to talk her out of driving home. I was sober. She wasn't. After enjoying the Friday night parties too much, on Saturday evening I had to stick to Cokes.

Outside in the parking lot, Kate insisted on driving. I argued with her. "You might kill yourself. You might kill someone else. You might get your license taken away. You might get thrown in jail." And when this wasn't getting to her, I said, "You might wreck your brand-new Miata."

After each of my suggestions, she repeated, "I don't care."

Eventually, she stormed by me. I made sure my feet weren't in the way. Quickly, I found Jack inside the bar, and he drove her to the Pleasant Inn, where she passed out.

At the end of that night, while I was still drinking Cokes with another crew member, Brad, Jack handed me the key to Kate's Miata convertible.

Brad followed me to the parking lot. I looked up at the stars and said, "Let's take her car for a ride."

The Pleasant Inn was approximately two miles away. It took us three hours to get there. We drove through every street to find the steepest hill. Until I got all four wheels off the ground, I wasn't going home.

Brad yelled as we flew over the hill, "You're going to wreck her car!"

I yelled over the speakers in the headrests, "I hate her."

"Well, don't kill us. Why do you hate her?" Brad held onto the dashboard as I continued my Mario Andretti impersonation.

"Last month she stomped on my foot, on purpose at the Edgartown Yacht Club."

"Maybe it was a mistake," Brad yelled over the engine.

"No, she thinks Jack and I slept together. And I'm the only platonic girlfriend he has."

I drove the car to the end of the street and turned it around. Turning to Brad, I said, "You don't want to get on the wrong side of this girl." I floored the gas.

As the streets grew too quiet to drive so fast, we finished our tour of Marblehead. We then noticed Jack's maroon Jaguar parked in front of an unfamiliar house. Brad figured that Vicki probably lived there. The lights were out, so we made one more stop.

After a small purchase from a late-night store,

we drove back to Jack's car and covered every inch of his maroon Jaguar with six rolls of toilet paper. We wrapped the windshield wipers and the wheel spokes. We took the last two rolls, opened the windows, and wrapped the roof from inside to out, around and around. We changed the color of the car from maroon to white. The neighborhood was quiet and the hour late; we almost burst our insides trying to keep from laughing too loudly.

When we returned to the inn, I joined Kate in the double bed. Brad took the couch as we laughed and laughed.

At one point, Kate rolled over, still drunk, and murmured, "Who are you and where am I?" We roared with laughter as she fell back to sleep.

Within a few hours, Jack drove into the parking lot of the inn with trails of white toilet paper flowing from his maroon Jaguar. Brad and I subdued our laughter as Jack entered the room.

"What happened to your car?" we asked, trying to keep our faces straight.

"You wouldn't believe it. This morning when I came out of a house, my car was completely covered with toilet paper. I think some kids did it."

Brad and I wouldn't look at each for fear of laughing.

Jack continued, "So I asked this cop for directions, and the cop said, 'The Pleasant Inn is up on your left. And by the way, congratulations.'"

Brad and I went into hysterics and awoke Kate from the dead. We looked out toward the red Miata and the maroon Jaguar with trails of white toilet paper.

Three months later at a bar in Boston, Kate walked up to me. I moved my feet.

She smiled and said, "Spurr, someone told me what you did to my Miata last August. It's the funniest thing I've ever heard." We shared a drink as I told her the tale of that summer night.

Years later, Kate and I have grown to become good friends. She is married and living in Colorado, and I visit her when I'm out there visiting my aunt. She consults and wins huge cases for Jack, and now drives a blue Mercedes. She once let me drive her husband's antique blue 1959 Porsche convertible, but he doesn't know that.

LOW TIDE TIMES

When was the last time you felt a warm breeze while driving either in a convertible with the top down or in a car with all the windows open?

Why not ask a friend who owns a convertible to go for a ride, or rent a convertible for the day on a whim?

How about renting a convertible during your next warm-weather vacation?

Is the extra cost of a convertible worth the experience per day?

Have you ever done a good deed for someone you know or someone you didn't know?

<u>**Spurr's tips:**</u>
To rent a convertible, Google travel discount companies. Bid a low price a few weeks before your trip. Discounts are more limited during vacation weeks.

Can You Help us Take Our Top Off?

Finding a parking space on Martha's Vineyard in July is like trying to find parking in New York City, and I needed a space for seventy-two hours. I took my friend Kelly's Jeep over on the ferry before our vacation began, so I could make a few sales calls around the tiny town of Vineyard Haven. Kelly and I had reserved a cottage in Edgartown, on the other side of the Vineyard.

Slowly, I drove the Jeep toward the harbor, and there it appeared: a seventy-two-hour parking space. There was even a sign, "72-HOUR PARKING." I locked the Jeep and jumped aboard a friend's boat to sail over to Falmouth to meet Kelly.

Kelly, never a worrier, kept saying, "When we get back to the Vineyard, I want to take the hard top off the Jeep, but it may be too heavy for us to lift."

"We'll take the roof off for the whole week," I told her.

"But what if it rains?"

"It will be sunny for the rest of our lives."

After sailing for two days, we caught the Vineyard ferry, checked into our cottage, and drove to the yacht club. During regattas, a non-member is allowed into the club if he or she is part of a crew. Some of the clubs are less friendly than others. My favorite ploy is to say in a loud voice, "I've been thrown out of better yacht clubs than this."

The Edgartown Yacht Club parking lot was filled with dozens of cars and sailors who were unloading gear for the sixty-seventh Annual Edgartown Regatta. Many of the boats had vans, which carried sailing gear, equipment, and extra sails. Some of the better sailing programs had the boat name painted on the van and sometimes a ten to seventy-foot motorboat to match.

I noticed a blue van with the name Drumbeat painted on the side and several men next to it.

"Kelly, drive up beside this blue van."

I leaned out of the window. "Excuse me, gentlemen, but could you help us take our top off?"

Every man in the parking lot dropped his gear and turned toward our Jeep. I smiled and held up a screwdriver and wrench. The Jeep top came off that sunny week, we met, talked with, and ate lunch or dinner with thirty-eight men. Kelly married one of them.

Years later, Kelly and I still share great laughs. I could have fun with her at a tax audit. We once decided with another neighbor, Diane, to take a one-night course at the local middle school. It was called "Shower Singing, for people who are afraid to sing in the shower." We came equipped with our shower caps but didn't take them out until after the first break. The other adults who took the course ranged from a retired couple who wanted to travel across the country and sing to a part-time opera singer. The songs the teacher chose ranged from "My Favorite Things" to "Somewhere Over the Rainbow." Each of us took a turn getting up and singing with the teacher as she played the piano. We all struggled, even the part-time opera singer.

Even now, years later, whenever I run into that retired couple shopping or walking through town, we sing, "Hello."

Kelly and I once got together while I was on business in New York City. It was a cold day and we decided to have tea at the Plaza Hotel. We walked by a street musician who was playing "Somewhere Over the Rainbow" on his saxophone. As the cold January wind blew her blonde hair, Kelly gave me a look and smiled. We entered the Plaza as most people did that day: windblown and freezing. We were led to a table inside the Palm Garden Restaurant, took off our coats, and rubbed our hands as we tried to get warm.

A violinist played at the tables nearby. As we looked at the huge menus, the violinist came toward our table and played "Somewhere Over the Rainbow."

Kelly put down her menu and said, "Spurr, don't sing." I sat and laughed and added this moment to the great catalog of memories that I have with Kelly.

LOW TIDE TIMES

Is there an island that you have always wanted to visit? Why?

Have you thought about going to your island paradise off-season when rates are lower?

Have you considered visiting a retreat or spa close to home?

Have you ever found an incredible parking space?

Have you driven a Jeep or other vehicle along a sandy beach? Where? What did it feel like?

<u>Spurr's tips:</u>
Go to a travel agent, get brochures on the place that you always wanted to go to, create a collage of that place, and put it somewhere that you see it everyday.

www.mvy.com

Convertible Ride to the Top of the World

"You must rent a convertible. It's the best way to see Maui," a business associate suggested.

I drive 30,000 miles a year for my job in sales. Avis couldn't pay me to drive during my vacation. Luckily, while attending the Maui Writers Conference, I not only found a convertible but also its owner, someone who would become a longtime friend. Chris lives in Honolulu but visits Maui often. After the last lecture of the conference, he found me, and we drove to the top of the Haleakala Crater.

We packed the convertible with towels, clothing and food, but nothing prepared me for being so close to heaven, or the 55-degree drop in temperature. Many people told me I had to do the sunrise bike ride down the 10,000-foot mountain, which begins at 3 a.m. The only time I get up that early is to go to the bathroom or catch a Delta flight!

The sun slid into the clouds, setting down toward the shores of Lahaina. I wore a windbreaker, two tops, green pants, socks, and sneakers, more clothes than I had worn all summer. I also wrapped two towels around my waist.

Moving from 95 degrees at the beach to 40 degrees on top of the crater, the temperature felt like it was Boston in the wintertime. My hands went numb. To get warm, I strutted along the lava rocks, faking a fashion show while dressed in white hotel towels. Tourists wondered if they were observing a Hawaiian tradition or if they should be running away.

According to legend, there is a quick green flash when the sun sets on the water. As the sun hit the water, the only green flash was my pants running toward the warmth of the convertible. Chris followed, started the engine, turned on the heat, and put the top up. With the fashionable white towels still around me, I started breathing again.

When the sky looked like black velvet, we folded the Mustang top down. The heat was turned on full blast, and the sky sparkled like Tiffany's best jewelry. If my fingers were longer, I could have touched the Big Dipper. The dictionary doesn't have words to describe this brilliant display of heaven. If your travel plans take you to the top of Maui, bring gloves.

As reality and the dropping temperatures called Chris and me back to sea level, we slowly drove down the dark curved road. We yelled up toward the sky, "It's the Big Dippa," with Chris using the Boston accent I had taught him earlier that day.

Along the way we saw the dark outline of grazing cows, which shared the mountainside with eucalyptus trees and the unique Hawaiian vegetation. One turn almost brought us head-on with a black cow. We could have had carpaccio!

Chris and I kept in contact for a year. He sent me his screenplay to critique, and I sent him my essays. We counted the days until the next Maui Writers Conference.

Before the next conference, we sat by the pool and brainstormed about future writing goals. We joked about becoming best-selling authors, renting the suite on the top floor of the Grand Wailea Hotel, and hanging our dirty laundry over the balcony. After that trip, we lost track of each other, but I will never forget his Aloha Spirit.

Years later, we almost walked into each other in Maui. Our friendship picked up right where it had left off, by the pool, and we still joke about hanging dirty laundry on the top floor of the Grand Wailea Hotel.

LOW TIDE TIMES

Have you stopped recently to watch the sunset?

When was the last time you watched the stars come out?

Have you ever watched the moon rise over the ocean, a lake, or a harbor?

While on vacation, have you done something adventurous?

If you are afraid to go on an adventure, why not ask a friend to join you, research it on the Internet, or take a course?

Spurr's tips:
www.outwardbound.com

www.grownupcamps.com

www.llbean.com

Outdoor Discovery Schools

SUMMERTIME AGGRAVATIONS

Do Tourists Leave Their Brains at Home?

How to Blow up a Gas Grill

Second Best Place to Get

Water Out of Your Ear

Do Tourists Leave Their Brains at Home?

Once again, I'm at the wheel of my car, caught behind an oversized vehicle filled with suitcases, two cats, and a boatload of people. Tourists! Tourists from all over the USA are in front of me riding their brakes. The brake lights glare red again and again and again. I think they're flashing S.O.S. If I were playing Jeopardy, I would say, "I'll take Aggravating Tourists for $200, Alex." I picture these people getting ready for vacation with their list of things to do:

1. Remove rearview mirrors.
2. Disconnect signaling blinkers.
3. Take brains out and leave in mailbox.

During July and August, I deal with a lot of vacationers, since my sales career takes me to many New England seashore resorts.

Before one sales call, I decided to designate these relaxing rovers by bird names, because they act like birdbrains. I sell women's accessories to boutiques and sometimes carry three ten-pound bags on my shoulders. One day in Maine, I was making my way down a crowded sidewalk when a Blind-sighted Warbler walked right into me.

I love it when I'm struggling with many bags, trying to open a door, and some Pelican says, "Those look heavy."

"Yes, they are," I say. "Would you like to help, or make comments?" One actually got up to help.

Later, while driving, I sighted several Terns slamming on their brakes on a major highway or crossing over four lanes of traffic to exit. I wanted to read my bird book and see if these birds would be extinct if they didn't make it to Exit 17. Probably.

My favorite birds belong to the Penguin family. They're usually spotted walking and taking up the entire sidewalk. They are best known for sudden stops while looking around, without any warning. What would the world be like if tourists walked and looked at the same time?

One July morning, trying to get a cup of coffee, I stood in line while a group of Waffling Waxwings tried to decide what to drink. One might think this decision would change their entire lives. A Common Tail Coin Pecker at the front of the line tried to use every coin in her purse, only to discover she was a penny short.

When I asked a number of people their opinions for this chapter, their eyes opened as wide as a Peacock's tail. Here's a checklist to help avoid oblivious birds while on vacation:

1. If children (young birds) kick your airline seat and the parents (older birds) are unconscious, stare back with a very serious look. This works well, particularly on the Speckled Mouse bird.

2. When loud birds such as the Southern Crested Screamer decide to sit almost on top of you at the beach, speaking many four-letter words at a high volume can help them seek a new nest.

3. If you are behind a van with wooden panels on the sides, park your car. You'll never get by it. These birds are known as Blue-footed Boobies.

4. If you're in a long line for coffee, go thirsty or pay for the drink that the tourist can't decide on.

5. Watch out for birds with large writing on their sweatshirts, telling you where they flew last year. They are known as the Wandering Albatrosses.

They usually can be spotted eating ice cream and dropping it.

6. A driver hitting the brakes often is tapping out Morse code. Keep the Morse code book in your car. This is particularly true of the Spotted Woodpecker.

If any of you wonder, yes, I have been on the road too long and for too many miles. I wish I were on vacation. I'm just a Lapland Longspurr.

LOW TIDE TIMES

Do you wish you could plan a vacation and not drive?

Have you ever been jealous when you see other people on vacation?

When waiting in a long line, do you get frustrated, or watch what is around you to appreciate the moment?

While on vacation, have you ever spoken to a fun group of strangers?

Have you kept in touch with someone you met on vacation?

<u>Spurr's tips:</u>
Laugh.

www.birdersworld.com

How to Blow Up a Gas Grill

Recently, my good friends Kelly and Dan purchased a high-tech Lynx gas grill.

Over a dozen years ago, I introduced Dan to Kelly at the Edgartown Regatta on Martha's Vineyard. Kelly and I have a bad habit of beating a joke into the ground for days, months, and sometimes years. We'll sing, or try to sing, the same Broadway tune over and over, but we never remember the words.

One day Kelly and I finished a beach chair therapy day across the street from their home and sat on their deck.

Dan walked outside and said, "Kelly, let me show you how to use the new grill."

She turned toward me. "Spurr, I don't have my

glasses. You'd better watch this with me."

Dan, an engineer, analyzed the buttons. With the cover closed, he directed us. "First, you turn this back valve on." He slowly walked to the front of their sparkling silver grill. "Then you turn this button on." Dan turned toward us, making sure we were paying attention. "Lastly, turn this on." With that twist of the valve, there was a huge BOOM.

Kelly grabbed me, dragged me off their two-foot deck and laughed hysterically into my shoulder.

Nothing happened to the grill or to us.

Dan ignored our laughter and the boom and said, "I have to drop something off at a friend's house. Put on the steaks, and I'll be back in ten minutes."

After he left, I asked Kelly, "Do you have any black face paint?"

Since Halloween is my favorite holiday, I assume everyone has black face paint, wigs, and assorted costumes stored in their front hall closet. I own as many Halloween items as Christmas decorations.

Kelly looked confused. "No, but I have black shoe polish." She ran downstairs to find it. I found hairspray in the bathroom cabinet and sprayed my bangs straight up as the steaks sizzled outside on the grill.

She applied the black shoe polish over her face and said, "Hey, it makes my teeth look whiter."

I applied some.

She coached me. "You don't have enough on. Put on more."

Just then, we heard Dan drive into the garage. Kelly and I ran outside and grabbed a newspaper to hide our faces. We stood with our backs to the door. Dan came out on the deck, and we turned toward him. "Dan, we had to re-light the grill." Dan paused, then doubled over laughing.

We ate dinner still wearing the shoe polish. The three of us kept laughing. After dinner, we decided to go to the other side of town to visit our good friend Gene, who had terminal cancer. Gene loved to listen to the police scanner and would tell us many of the events left out of the Marblehead Reporter's police log.

When I first moved to this small town, Kelly told me to always wave to the cops and get to know them, in case you needed them or in case they stopped you. Since Marblehead, a town of 20,000, is so difficult to drive to, there isn't a lot of crime. The Marblehead Police are a great group of people who help make this town safe.

Some of the highlights of the police log have included: a seagull walked on the sidewalk, a skunk had a tuna can stuck on his head, damage was done to a rope, and a car was stopped for having too many tinted windows. It is the best nonfiction written weekly.

That night as we drove home to Gene's house, we

stopped at an intersection. A policeman I knew from the coffee shop saw us, looked into my car, waved, and said, "Nice teeth."

Kelly and I keep a picture of us that was taken in Gene's kitchen. Gene is no longer with us, but our blackened faces brought him a smile.

LOW TIDE TIMES

When was the last time you had a barbecue or attended one?

Could you convince a friend to host a barbecue and bring the main course?

Do you dress up on Halloween? Why not?

When was the last time you went to a costume party?

Why not host a dinner party with masks?

<u>Spurr's tips:</u>
Go buy a mask and wear it.

www.masksoftheworld.com

www.anytimecostumes.com

The Second Best Place to Get Water Out of Your Ear

After a day of fully enjoying the 2,000 feet of connected pools, slides, waterfalls, and rapids at the Grand Wailea Resort, my right ear was filled with water.

Ear blockage is not the worst thing that could happen while on Maui, but after frolicking with frozen drinks in the floating bar, and then in the waves of the Pacific, and even jumping up and down on one foot, the water was still in there.

I walked around the pools, Jacuzzis, and fountains. I walked up the stairs, under the white plumeria trees, and back to the perfect beach chair at the Hibiscus Pool. I wanted to ask the waitress to help me get the water out of my ear. Instead, I ordered a frozen drink and savored the moment with the palm trees swaying in tandem with the ocean waves. Only I couldn't hear anything!

During dinner that evening, I tried listening to a conversation between my friend Chris and Dave the bartender, but the water in my ear didn't help my hearing. Twice during dinner I got up, went to the ladies' room, made sure no one could see me, and jumped up and down to release the water. No luck.

After dinner Chris and I walked out into the award-winning gardens. *Travel & Leisure* magazine voted this resort the second most beautifully landscaped hotel in the world. I laughed and thought, "If this was the second best, what the hell did number one look like?"

I stopped Chris. "This is a strange request, but I can't get the water out of my ear. It's driving me crazy. In the past, I've had it released by a friend shaking my head. So will you shake my head?"

Chris looked at me, closed his eyes, shook his head, and said, "You want me to do what?"

Chris is over six feet tall and about twice my petite size. As he took hold of my head and gave it a couple of good shakes, the water finally released. We laughed, turned, and noticed a family of four standing behind us wondering if this was the Bates Motel from Alfred Hitchcock's 1960 movie, *Psycho*.

LOW TIDE TIMES

Have you ever had water in your ear or up your nose and couldn't get it out?

Were you having fun before you got water in your ear?

Do you unblock your ears in a unique way?

Have you ever had a funny experience while trying
to get water out of your ear?

Did you have this experience with a friend? If so, when was the last time you and your friend laughed about it?

Spurr's tips:
Call that friend or mail a card.

www.ehow.com

www.health911.com

DRESSING FOR SUMMER

Flip-Flops

Goodbye Lilly

Swimming at Wedding Receptions

Flip-Flops

Before I bought my first pair of flip-flops, or "slippas," as they are referred to in Hawaii, I never understood why people wore them. They looked uncomfortable with that thong separating the big toe from the other toes and no back or top for support.

My sailing buddies wore flip-flops during regattas. I couldn't figure out how they could run around on board, pulling in lines and sails, and how they kept their balance on a wet deck while they wore flip-flops. Maybe the fact that they wore these shoes was one reason why we only captured a few trophies.

Then one day while shopping at Sears, I almost walked by a pair of lime-green-and-white

Sperry flip-flops. I popped my foot out of my shoe, dropped one of the flip-flops on the floor, and glided my foot into nirvana.

Immediately, I slipped the salesgirl my credit card and forever walked in freedom. I wore those flip-flops until they broke apart.

Now, years later, when I think of that pair of summer slippas, I miss them. What could be better than open toes and heels?

Flip-flops represent independence to me—and the freedom to wear summer clothes. This freedom includes doing without a coat, hat, gloves, or scarf. My feet look forward to being open to the world. Just remembering those summer slippas makes me want to take a deep breath and think of the day when I will have the liberty of open toes again.

I read somewhere that a Johns Hopkins University study revealed that the right foot goes "flip" and the left goes "flop." I visualized professors dressed in corduroy jackets doing research while they walked around campus wearing flip-flops. Did the entire faculty and student body walk around wearing them? The echo of "flip-flop" throughout campus must have created an atmosphere unlike any other on earth.

I love walking on a summer night while wearing flip-flops. I hear the trees rustling their leaves. I feel the warm summer breezes as I listen to the staccato beat of my summer shoes. It's as musical a part of summer as the chirp of crickets.

In *Travel & Leisure* of August 2002, there was a feature entitled "33 Ways to Make Summer Last." I was lulled into summer when I opened that issue. The 33 Ways included renting a convertible, riding a roller coaster, having clambakes, and eating ice cream.

One section listed places to stay where the dress code is barefoot. Since I love flip-flops, going barefoot is almost too much of an escape for me. If I went barefoot for a week, I probably would never return to New England, where I need to wear socks and shoes for most of the year.

When people learn of my love for summer, they don't understand why I've continued to live in New England. Well, it's home. I would miss the big, colorful maple trees in autumn; Copley Square's Trinity Church during the December candlelight ceremony; and the beauty of sunsets on the brick buildings in the Back Bay section of Boston. Still, when autumn comes, I'm sad that my toes will be covered up during those long, cold winters. Although I long for a warm wave to slap me in the face, at that time of year a fleece jacket and cotton turtleneck are almost as comfortable as flip-flops. In late spring or early fall, I've been known to wear both flip-flops and fleece. For a Yankee gal like me, it's fuzzy freedom.

At one sales call, I asked a client who was sporting a turquoise pair of flip-flops, "Judy, I love your shoes. I want to buy a new pair, but I'm wondering, how many flip-flops are too many?"

She smiled. "I have fourteen pairs, a pair to go with every outfit. I once had a pair of shoes, back in the '70s. I named them Platypus."

Being of a competitive nature, I now had to do some serious retail therapy. The next day I found a pair of light-blue flip-flops at a Reebok outlet. They were a sporty style that reminded me of my first Sperry pair.

Since that first Sears purchase, I buy a new pair each year. The best thing about flip-flops? They're cheap. At last count, I had five pairs: a pair of black-and-pink Nikes; a black pair with little cloth daisies; a pair with turquoise-colored stones (featured in O Magazine); and, of course, white flip-flops, and a pair from Hawaii, with blue palm trees etched on top of the white soles. This pair cushions my feet like the sand on the beach and was a bargain at $5.99. I've found that the thicker the sole, the more comfortable the flip-flop.

A problem arises each summer: one pair becomes my favorite because of its fashion or comfort. The $5.99 Hawaiian pair was my favorite one summer because they are the most comfortable. Sometimes I wear my favorite shoes so much that they wear out, and then the biggest stress is to find a proper replacement.

Pedicures are a part of the flip-flop

experience, not just for color but also for the foot massage. I had my first pedicure at age forty, and now I'm hooked. The morning after the pedicure, when I woke up and saw my toes painted red, I almost jumped out of bed, thinking that my feet were bleeding. I quickly switched to a light pink color. A few years ago while on vacation, a group of friends and I painted our toes light blue. No males were included in this experiment. Blue toes worked well while on vacation, but when I returned to Boston, I had to switch back to pink. We are so straight in New England.

In December, my flip-flops are stored in a cedar chest with my summer wardrobe. I often want to put them on and wear them around the house. But what I want more is to wear my slippas on a warm beach, and have the hot sand flip up on the backs of my legs. The winter winds won't allow me to wear them right now. I'll wait until I know that I'm booked on my next warm-weather vacation. Perhaps I'll create a new tradition when I take out those shoes: The Opening of Flip-Flop Season.

LOW TIDE TIMES

What are your favorite summer clothes?

Are there some that make you feel like summer as soon as you see or touch them?

Is there somewhere you have a great memory while wearing them?

Spurr's tips:
www.abcstores.com - for the best pair of flip-flops.

Goodbye Lilly

Have you heard of Lilly Pulitzer? She designed that signature clothing of the sixties: the preppy dresses in hot pinks and lime green worn to yacht clubs by women who wore headbands even while taking a shower.

I read in *The Boston Globe* that Jackie Kennedy, Rose Kennedy, Amy Vanderbilt, and more recently Brooke Shields have worn these ridiculous bright fashions, but for most of my life, I wouldn't wear Lilly clothes to the grand opening of an outhouse. I thought the women who wore Lilly were stuck in a fashion time warp. But as I gained speed into my forties and my friends built their wardrobes buying Lillys, I finally surrendered.

During the late fifties, Lilly Pulitzer became

bored with just being a Palm Beach socialite. Married to Peter Pulitzer of the publishing family, she started selling juice at a stand, squeezing oranges from the groves her husband owned. The O.J. stained her clothing, so Lilly bought brightly colored print fabric at Woolworth's and asked a seamstress to create sleeveless dresses. The busy prints hid the stains. Some women bought more of the dresses than they did the juice.

In the eighties, when fashion trends became more formal, Lilly declared bankruptcy. A decade later, she licensed her name to Jim Bradbeer and his partners.

In *The Boston Globe* article, reporter Suzanne Ryan wrote, "To wear Lilly then was a status symbol. It wasn't the price tag (moderate) for the loud pink sundresses or the golf pants decorated with apple-green palm trees that were significant. The very fact that you knew about Lilly meant you were part of an exclusive circle. You were a debutante. You attended an Ivy League school. You had a trust fund. You were a member of a restricted social club. You wintered in Palm Beach and summered on Nantucket. You wore Lilly."

Well, I only attended an Ivy League school to drink and meet Dartmouth fraternity boys. I wish I had wintered in Palm Beach and had a trust fund, but the closest I came to being a debutante was living on Nantucket for a summer.

One summer, I finally found it necessary to buy a Lilly. I couldn't bring myself to shell out $150 on a pair of pants or $90 for shorts, but I considered a dress an investment. In my Massachusetts North Shore hometown, more and more of my friends were wearing Lilly dresses. When they first started wearing those "obnoxious bright things," I thought, "You couldn't drag me through a mud puddle to make me wear a Lilly."

One of my college girlfriends, who was an expert at finding Dartmouth fraternity boys, told me that the word Lilly is always hidden in the fabric. It's on the lobster tail of my newest investment. This secret signature is something like finding a hidden treasure in a *Highlights* children's magazine you might have read while visiting the dentist.

When I entered the Lilly Shop on Nantucket, I had to reach for sunglasses. The walls were bright white, and most of the clothing was bright pink. There was a huge selection of pants, shorts, tops, sweaters, dresses, purses, and shoes. Shoppers are thrown out of the store if they wear black.

During this June day, I tried on various Lilly items, creating a one-woman fashion show for my Nantucket man, who waited outside on the Lilly-covered couch. I handed the woman behind the counter my "American Distress" card and signed into a new fashion stage of life. As I carried the white-handled shopping bag out of the Lilly store, I walked with a new confidence. I was now that woman I had seen for years, gliding in and out of the yacht clubs—except for the headband, that is.

My bag was filled with periwinkle-blue lobsters and crabs, which were also highlighted on my lime-green dress. My dress had a ruffled-edge top with spaghetti straps that tied into small bows. Everything Lilly usually had a bow somewhere. It remains one of the most comfortable dresses I own, with a flexible gathered back and a soft white cotton lining. The cotton is so soft it probably was grown at prep schools and picked by the professors.

When I wore my Lilly to a restaurant that night, my Nantucket man and I ate at a romantic corner table. I felt beautiful. Most of the night, my date sat across the room at the piano, tickling the ivories instead of me. I had just spent $150 on this Lilly, and he preferred Steinway. I must have lost my mind for part of that summer. This Nantucket man didn't even like spending the day at the beach, let alone appreciate Beach Chair Therapy.

At the end of the summer and that short-lived relationship, my three girlfriends and I had a Lilly party. All the women and a few sophisticated men were dressed in those famous pinks and greens. All the napkins and decorations—an extra-large blow-up beach ball and scallop shell—were all pink and green. The Lilly showroom in New York lent us a quilt made entirely of vintage Lilly fabric. We made fake preppy name tags with names such as Sea Shell and Pinky. The outdoor party lasted late into the warm August night.

At 4 a.m. the next day, I flew off to my second Maui Writers Conference. Although I was still paying "American Distress" for my first Maui trip, the Maui experience is like wearing a Lilly—some things in life just can't be passed up.

On Labor Day, as I stretched out my white-shoe days to the limit, I sat wearing my Lilly and writing in my journal. The conference had been another investment in memories. It seemed very appropriate to be dressed in lobsters and crabs while at a seafood restaurant named after the Hawaiian state fish, Humuhumunukunukuapua'a. I was sad to be saying goodbye to summer and so long to my Lilly. Maybe next June, "American Distress" will bring me another Lilly.

LOW TIDE TIMES

Have you ever bought clothing that was a different style from your usual wardrobe?

Are you afraid to wear something different?

Would it be uncomfortable for you?

Would you go to a store and try this clothing on?

What are some of your favorite pieces of clothing?

<u>Spurr's tips:</u>
www.lillypulitzer.com

Swimming at Wedding Receptions

Instead of catching the bouquet at an early September wedding, I caught a sailboat ride that the wedding party will never forget. The couple, Keith and Victoria, had picked a perfect day for their wedding. During the reception, a group of us sailed a boat from a nearby harbor over to a yacht club to pick up the bride and groom.

Four of us—Pete, Kathy, Candy, and I—sailed Pete's boat, Go-Go, finishing three bottles of champagne during the hour-long trip. Soon after, Kathy and Candy needed to use the head. It was a feat in itself to be sailing aboard a racing boat, dressed for a wedding, let alone balance below deck to use the head.

I told the girls, "I'll show you how to go by sitting on the lifelines and peeing overboard." I pulled up the back of my long yellow dress and blazer and sat on the lifelines on the edge of the boat. This is similar to sitting on a narrow fence. Given the motion of the boat and consumption of large quantities of champagne, it requires the balance of a circus tightrope walker.

Squatting over the lifelines, I then did a back flip into the water.

The captain, Pete, yelled to his crew, "Quick, grab the life-ring!" The crew scrambled to get it and throw it into the water.

The next thing I knew, I was looking up at bubbles, confused. Where were the bubbles coming from? The lifelines were not the taut type I was used to on larger racing boats. I guess lifelines are called that so people who drink several glasses of champagne won't sit on them and try to pee.

As my junior lifesaving swimming lessons kicked in and I surfaced, I yelled, "Screw the life-ring, I know how to swim—get the camera!"

My sailing companions pulled me on board. My yellow dress and linen blazer were drenched.

As I climbed on board, I said, "I wish I had seen that. It must have been hysterical."

My dress dried before we reached the dock of the yacht club. The blazer lasted another season. Only Ann Taylor stores could sell clothing perfect for every occasion, even for a wedding reception harbor swim.

Six years later the groom's mother, Lois, told

me that during the wedding, she had been watching the boat through binoculars from the yacht club deck, where she sat with her brothers and sisters. When she saw me hit the water, she yelled, "Woman overboard!" They all saw the splash, and I surfaced like a well-dressed mermaid. I didn't know it at the time, but Lois and her siblings were grieving over the death of one of their brothers forty-eight hours earlier. His last request had been for the family to attend Keith and Victoria's wedding. My peeing demonstration lightened their day.

A week after this conversation with Lois, I made copies of the photos of me dripping aboard Go-Go and presented them to her. I gave her a card filled with the pictures and entitled, "Woman overboard!"

Victoria and Keith have become great friends. They adopted two of the most beautiful blond little boys in America. Since the adoptions were in the United States, each one was a difficult process. Several times at the last minute, the birth mother had decided to keep her baby, and Victoria and Keith had come home empty-handed. But after their first adoption they told all their friends, "Life is a journey, not a destination." I try to remember that philosophy as much as possible.

One recent December, Victoria, Keith, and their first son were away from home for a month in Florida, trying to finish the adoption procedures and bring their second son home. Their friends planned a big homecoming for that day with posters, gifts, and food. In the freezing cold wind, I tied blue ribbons to their fence until I ran out of ribbon.

When I picked up Keith, Victoria, and sons at the airport, it was one of the coldest days of the year. I was nervous driving Keith's brand-new Jeep Cherokee, and because of the new security measures, I couldn't wait in my car outside the baggage claim area. I finally found a place to park the Jeep and waited for my cell phone to ring. I wanted to be sure they didn't have to wait outside in the cold, especially with a newborn.

My phone finally rang: "We'll get our luggage and be outside in five minutes," Keith said.

Three minutes later, I couldn't wait any longer. I drove up and didn't see them. The state police officer waved me on. I looked and looked for my friends. The trooper, who was wearing those high leather boots, waved again. Then he came up to my car, "Lady, you have to move."

I held my hands in a folded prayer position. "My friends just called me and are coming out."

"No. You have to move." He continued to wave the other traffic on.

"Please you don't understand. They have a brand-new baby and have been in Florida for a month."

The trooper looked at me, as if to say, "I haven't heard that one before."

"Please, they are coming out right now. They just called me. They are coming out."

"If you can't see them, you have to move."

I started getting upset, "They're right there." I thought I would get into a fistfight with the trooper.

Finally, I saw Keith's tanned face rolling the largest filled luggage rack I've ever seen. "There they are!" I jumped out of the car, leaving the door open (the trooper must have loved that) and greeted Keith with huge hugs. I asked him where the rest of his family was.

"Inside. We didn't want the baby to get cold," he replied. I ran inside the terminal, while Keith loaded up his car. I ran around about ninety people waiting for their luggage and found Victoria, their first son, and their new son. I led them outside, while holding the older son's hand.

We settled into the packed car. As we were about to drive away, the trooper asked, "Where's the baby?" Victoria held him up to the window.

It no longer seemed like the coldest day of the year.

A few weeks later, Victoria and I and all our girlfriends watched the last episode of *Sex And The City* together. In that final episode, after months of frustration, one of the characters and her husband are disappointed once again because an adoption has fallen through. I suddenly realized that this situation was similar to Victoria's. As she sat on the couch and I sat on the floor, I grabbed her leg and held it. We all cried, realizing that sometimes even television can reflect our lives.

LOW TIDE TIMES

When was the last time you went swimming with your clothes on?

Have you ever gone swimming without your clothes on?

When was the last time you went swimming on the spur of the moment?

Did you ever swim at night? Where?

Have you gone in the water lately, either indoors or outdoors?

Spurr's tips:
Go swimming.

Take time with friends, even to pick them up at the airport.

BEACH WITHDRAWAL

A New England Dock

That Summer Day

Surfing Again

A New England Dock

O ne silent summer morning, I climbed down the cool gray flagstone steps with a steaming cup of coffee and beach bag in hand. The gangplank was my bridge to the dock: a flat twenty-by-thirty-inch piece of thick pine with six steel cleats that hold the boat lines. I pulled out my faded green canvas beach chair from under the gangplank and set it on the edge of the dock, facing out toward the end of the harbor. I kicked away the empty shells left by hungry seagulls. I listened for their "plunk" and watched their slow deep descent into the ocean. I put out a fluffy white towel for my feet.

The blue harbor stretched to the horizon in front of me, filled with dozens of blue-and-white boat hulls secured to moorings. The waves rocked me slowly into the quiet rhythm of a summer morning. I applied coconut suntan lotion.

On that early morning, it was already 80 degrees. The hot winds touched the back of my neck.

I sat and wrote, entirely inspired, and phrase after phrase filled my blue-lined journal pages, stained with suntan lotion. Magazines from my beach bag flapped in the wind, forgotten until I finished writing.

White sailboat jibs were raised and lowered. Boats hummed back and forth to other docks. At times I put down my journal and jumped into the cold, deep harbor, then climbed back up the mussel-shell-covered stone steps.

At the end of October, the dock is moved to its winter home, on the beach up harbor, corraled with the other docks. Some days, I jog by to say hello.

One winter Sunday, I jogged by the docks and jumped up on that familiar pine deck, kicking the snow and wishing the white flakes were the seagulls' shells of summer.

While the winds blew around me, I exhaled. My breath became part of the scene. I closed my eyes and wished I were back on my beach chair with journal in hand. Instead, I felt the snow and cold biting into my body, reminding me I had to wait.

As I jumped down, I realized this was more than a dock. The dock was a comfort zone, a place I go to be inspired to write. This dock was my white-carpeted space, my summer place—the island of my inspiration.

LOW TIDE TIMES

Is there a place you remember that brought you peace?

When was the last time you returned to that spot?

Do you know when your life is too hectic?

Could you plan a long weekend housesitting?

Why not schedule an hour-long walk each day?

<u>**Spurr's tips:**</u>
Go back to that peaceful place, or find one like it.

Call a friend to housesit at an oceanfront home.

Plan a long walk.

That Summer Day

Twenty or more years ago, two years after I'd finished college, I decided to goof off and spend the summer working on the island of Nantucket. I knew in my heart that if I didn't take the time then, someday I would regret it.

Now, years later, I only regret not having more days like that special August day, that summer day when there were no clouds, no wind, and no need to hurry to be anywhere—when I could just be.

On Nantucket, I worked as a hostess at The Brotherhood of Thieves restaurant. My schedule allowed me to spend five days a week at Nobadeer Beach, a long stretch of sand dunes outlined by cliffs. Beach roses filled the air with summer scents; green dune grass quietly stirred parallel to waves in the sea.

That summer day, I left my beach towel, striped bag, and Coppertone suntan oil on the hot sand and walked. I strolled into the waves and walked on the sandy beach along the surf and close to the dunes.

Years later, if I close my eyes, I can still hear the waves and almost smell the beach roses. If I hold my breath and listen carefully, I can still hear the shells and stones retreating into the sea. Ah, if only I could go there now and run into the wet sand, jump into the waves, run up the dunes and leave everything behind.

On that August day, I walked and walked and walked, going nowhere without a care. I had no regard for time or even the abandonment of my beach bag. I couldn't remember if I had locked my bike. The sun beat blissfully on my back. My two-month-old bronze summer tan needed to be evened out.

On that island beach, I felt I could walk around and around and arrive back where I started, a feeling of freedom amid a sea of security. I let the waves splash me and caress me. I tumbled in them and let them take control. I rode those waves and let them throw me. Salt covered my body like dried candle wax. To be able to spend an unplanned, daylong walk on the beach was pure ecstasy.

For hours I walked, passing only a few people. There were dogs, happy, smiling dogs. Nantucket always has great dogs. No houses lined this shore, just miles of dunes. It seemed a different world there, just sea grass, dunes, waves, and me.

After a few hours, I reached the distant part of the island called Tom Nevers Head, where long, unmarked sandy roads lead to the top of the dunes and a few scattered cottages without electricity.

During my first trip to Nantucket the previous summer, in 1978, friends had brought me out to their cottage with similar-looking stairs. With the spontaneity of that day, I climbed those steps to their cottage. Maybe my friends had decided to leave their schedules and take advantage of that hot summer day. No one was in or around the cottage, but a car was there. I helped myself to a glass of water, left a note, and hoped to see my friends walking on the beach on my way back.

At the end of that summer I started my career, and since then I have never stopped and walked as I did that August day.

Twenty years later I found myself driving to a National Seashore beach. My sales appointment had taken me to Cape Cod. Warm air was finally breaking through a long icy winter. As I drove up to the empty beach parking lot, I saw an artist capturing the late afternoon spring light on a white canvas. I slid back in my seat to take off my navy knee-highs and shoes. I approached the sand; it was like an old friend that my feet were visiting again after almost nine months' absence. I walked up to the dunes and out to the beach. I stood, taking in the salty air, and found a weathered piece of driftwood to sit on. I brushed off the old driftwood and smiled at my caution.

I think often of that summer day twenty years ago. I dream of leaving my locked car and walking along the National Seashore for miles and miles. Now, I stop and watch the waves. I can almost feel them. They pull me in and out of too many sales calls, too much paperwork, and the ten telephone calls waiting to be returned before 5 p.m. I hold my arms for warmth as the afternoon sun fades. I look down at the miles of sand and dunes, still caked in winter cold. I look south and watch more waves stretch out to the endless sea. I remember and want to walk.

LOW TIDE TIMES

When was the last time you walked on a beach or around a lake?

Do you wear your watch while on vacation?

Have you ever wanted to sell all your belongings and move to a beach resort?

Where would that beach resort be?

Do you have plans to take an extended vacation for more than ten days? When are you going to plan that?

<u>Spurr's tips:</u>
Go for a walk on the beach.

www.nantucketchamber.org

www.nantucket.net

Surfing Again

August 2002. Charley's Cove, Kihei, Maui. 7 a.m. I'm on a green surfboard. As I paddle out into the warm Pacific, I see palm trees lining the shore, sapphire blue waves, and the distant islands. Jet lag flows over me after a twelve-hour flight and a short night's sleep. The puffy white clouds hang above as the gentle winds caress my tired back. The turquoise water reflects the sunshine. I am back. My smile surrounds the surfboard.

During the flight the day before, I played my Sony Walkman and listened to the song by the rock group U2. Now, whenever I hear that song played, I feel as if I'm back in Charley's Cove and surfing again.

The trip from Boston to Los Angeles and then

Maui exhausted and excited me. The long flight was worth the price of admission to paradise. Or in my case, 30,000 frequent-flyer miles.

One problem that forever plagues me is my carry-on luggage. My bag was filled with a bathing suit, nightgown, shorts, T-shirt, dress, laptop, portable printer, and toiletries. I always think my luggage might end up on board a space shuttle. Although Hawaii has stores where I could replace everything, shopping could make me lose precious beach time. If I could fit a folding surfboard in my carry-on, I would do it. I'll admit that I did pack twelve pairs of shoes for a ten-day vacation. But they were inside my fifty-pound checked bag.

One of the best places to people-watch is the Los Angeles airport, a.k.a. LAX, which is a unique experience, especially for a provincial Bostonian. I played a game called Celebrity-Look-Alike Contest.

On that two-hour layover at LAX, I saw a man who walked through the airport and looked like the exercise guru Richard Simmons. I thought, "He's the winner of the Richard Simmons Look-Alike Contest."

As he walked closer, a woman yelled out, "RICHARD!" With that, he waved. I recognized his famous striped shorts, his curly hair and smile. It figures I would see Richard Simmons, not Robert

Redford or Brad Pitt. No, I saw Richard Simmons.

On the final leg of the trip, the plane soared out over the Pacific: Destination Paradise.

Since I'm five foot two, I didn't mind being stuffed into the window seat. I used the time for writing, listening to tunes, and reading. There were no phones, faxes, or e-mails to distract me.

Ten hours later, I was on a green surfboard in 85-degree water, waiting for a set of waves, as the U2 song continued to play in my mind. Instead, I sang, "It's a beautiful wave." As I tried to paddle out, all the weightlifting I had done over the last three months wasn't enough to help my arm strength.

Charley's Cove is where many tourists learn the sport. The locals refer to it as "the cove." That day, a group of fifty-year-old surfers waited to ride the waves before going to work.

The scene reminded me of the Muffin Shop in my town, where a group of successful retired gentlemen meet, drink coffee, and solve the problems of the world.

To me, this was the Muffin Shop scene of Maui. The only thing these older surfers were missing were cups of coffee. Surfboards with drink holders? Why hasn't anyone thought of this? Here was my idea of a perfect coffee hour: lying on a surfboard, looking out at a calendar-cover view on a ten-day vacation, and knowing twelve pairs of shoes waited in my room.

Then a set of three-foot waves started. They were not frightening like the waves at Ho'okipa on the other side of the island, but gentle three-foot waves.

I thought about lying on the board, outside of the wave break, and taking a nap. It was quiet. Most of all, I wanted an imprint of the blue water, green palm trees, and the islands beyond etched in my brain forever. Thank you U2. Their music lingered in my mind. Suddenly my surf buddy Mikela yelled, "Janet, paddle!"

Behind me was a wave. I paddled. A surfer almost hit me as I lost my opportunity to catch the wave. Mikela soared in to shore. He paddled back to me as if he were being towed out on a Jet Ski. My arms hurt just watching him.

He sat on his board and said, "You have to give the other surfers the right of way. If you don't, they'll ride over your board."

I thought to myself, "Thank you for telling me this after our third time surfing." Instead, I said, "The surfer will ride over your board." I pointed down at the borrowed surfboard I sat on.

"Heads up." He turned his board like a sports car. I looked out at the wave and turned my board (or his board) as if I were moving a sleep sofa. I paddled but was lost behind the spindrift of the wave. I looked around, hoping I could find someone to paddle for me.

Mikela caught the second wave. I paddled to

catch the third. No luck. He paddled over, sensing my frustration. His brown eyes were warm and sparkling. His hair was slicked back from the water. His tanned skin was darker than the golden-brown sand on the shore. "You can just ride the wave on the surfboard like a boogie board. You don't have to stand up."

"Really?" Suddenly, it was an even more beautiful day.

Mikela let me use his smaller board this time, which was easier to maneuver. It was a lighter weight, but I still felt as if I were trying to paddle while on top of a twin bed. We waited in silence for another set of waves. The warm breeze touched my wet hair. I looked out toward the west Maui Mountains. So excited to have my feet in the Pacific again, I slapped the top of the water. Then a set came in. I was determined to ride a wave that day.

Mikela waited. "The third one looks good."

"How can you tell which wave will be good?"

He turned to me. "How can you tell a sales call is going well? Janet, after doing something for years, you just know."

Mikela waited while I decided to take his advice to go for a boogie-board ride on the surfboard. I paddled hard and after several attempts at floundering like a flounder, my board took off over the edge of the white crest. The sensation was sensual. The wave propelled me and captured my board with its power. The sound of the wave engulfed me, as if I were inside a Surround Sound theater. The board rode the wave. After about ten seconds of riding the surfboard while lying down, I decided to try standing up.

I concentrated on the tip of the board, aiming it straight into the shore. The palm trees ahead looked like exclamation points. Slowly, I rose and balanced with the motion of the ocean. I stood. My rubber windsurfing booties stuck to the waxed board like Super Glue. I kept riding as the wave continued. The wind almost lifted me toward shore.

People lined the shore waiting for their 8:00 a.m. surf lessons. I felt several pairs of eyes on me. I was standing, I was surfing, and it wasn't ending. I held out my arms, as if to say, "Well, is this wave ever going to end?"

I felt as comfortable on my surfboard as I did in my own living room. It was as if the wave and I were in a slow-motion movie and I was the water star. I kept surfing. I was Gidget; where was Moon Doggie?

I thought about what people must be saying on shore: "Boy, she's good."

Slowly, the wave ended. My board gently dropped below the surface. I jumped off into about two feet of water. I held onto my board and looked out again to Mikela, the Pacific, and the island beyond. It's a beautiful wave.

LOW TIDE TIMES

Go to the beach and bring a chair.

Acknowledgements

This book would not have ever been possible without the help of so many friends, mentors and teachers. I mostly want to thank my great friends in Marblehead, Massachusetts, especially Mary Boucher, who bought me my first book on writing, Forrest Rodts who painted me the best cover in the world and Brian Hancock, for his time as the layout design artist was outstanding. Roger Farrington thank you for your great photo on the back cover and Tyna Hull for your website magic.

My other Marblehead friends have also continued to support me in so many ways that I'm so proud to have them to come home to. There aren't enough words to say thank you for keeping me laughing in this special town.

To my mentors, teachers, friends and all the writers and people from the Maui Writers Conference, especially, Mitch Albom, Wally Amos, Jack Canfield, Rick Evans, Sam Horn, Dan Poynter, Ronda Rich, Melanie Rigney, Tom and Holly Sawyer, and Shannon Tullius. All these people have made such a difference in my life and I appreciate it.

My great friends from Maui who taught me the Aloha Spirit. John Ball who has been on this long publishing road with me. My Grand Wailea Resort friends, Marissa Hue and my surfing buddy.

Diana Ansley for that first summer day on the lake. Jen Babine. Jeff Barrows and his dock. The Baylor family. My beach gal friends, Amy, Cabby, Dana and Lisa. My business partner, Bethany and for all of my fantastic, fun clients and manufacturers, especially the people at Baked Beads. Deirdre Beyer, Dana Bisbee, Petra Breen and Bill Bryson.

My teachers at the Boston Center for Adult Education, Cambridge Center for Adult Education and Harvard Extension School and my tutor Andrew Szanton.

Everyone at Colby-Sawyer College, especially Peg Andrews, my alumni friends and the boys who hung out with us in front of Best Dorm. D.C. for helping me understand mortgages. Scot Channell. Lisa Connolly. Rita Corlett. Trevor Corson. The Rev. Lorne Coyle.

Dr. D. and Delta Airlines for frequent flyer miles. Dolphin Yacht club members. Sheila Duncan. Ron Durette for the greatest retail therapy night of my life.

Shilan Fine. Sally Fitt. The Foley Family, Fulvio, Norm Gautreau for telling me about the Maui Writers Conference, Richard Getz, God, Geraldine Gomery, Google, Jim Grace and John Grisham.

Christ Hartley. Gabi Herkett for being in line in back of me and being a great friend. Karen Horowitz for your time, efforts and friendship. Russ Jones and Ken Leonard.

The Larsons. My Lee Street neighbors, who still make me laugh. Richard LaMotte, Bud Lethbridge for my Colby-Sawyer scholarship. Jeff Levin.

My friends who came to Miami for my birthday, especially Kim and Mark Olson, D.T. and J.T. Denise and Bakerman, Connie Brown, Bill and Tracy Cotton, Liz Davies, Kate Fletcher, Kristin Mascio, Elyse Newhouse, and Dana Swezey.

The Marblehead Novelheaders book group. Gary Marchese, Maria, Charles, Billy Pilla and the Rev. Peter Wenner for taking care of my Dad. Monica Mania. Siobhan and Malachy McCourt, Shelly Mecum, the angel. Scot and Lorraine Miller. My Newport sailing buddy, Brian Cunha and Julie Snyder. Ramsey Myatt.

Patricia Nelson, Jean Noyes, Mary Noyes,

Carol Nyffenegger. NWU people including Chris Amner, Charles Coe and Barbara Beckwith.

Susan Orlean. Joel Osteen, Val Packard, Carmen Pastore, Suzanne Philips, Maureen Pratt. The Red Rock Writers Group, The Rice Family and Tucker, Fern Reiss. Holly Rich from Hunter Editions. Squire Rushnell.

St. Anthony for helping me to find things. All of the Schellers, Anthony Silva, Ben Sherwood, Virginia and Neil Schwartz, Virginia Joy Smith, Spirit of '76 Bookstore, the Spurr Family and my cousins. The staff at IRA Subaru, the staff at the Trapp Family Lodge, Rob Starr, Bruce Sullivan.

Everyone at Trinity Church Boston. Carole and Roger Tropf for snakes at the lake. Joe Tye's Spark Your Dream Workshop at the Grand Canyon.

John Whalen. Jacqueline Whitmore for wearing Lilly Pulitzer, Susan Wiggs and her husband, who knows how to bodysurf. John Voss for the Spurr of the Moment Column in your magazine.

Linda Weltner, Caitlin Williams, Diane and Ray Williams, Craig Wilson for your column every Wednesday in USA Today. Betty Wright. the Wisdom House in Litchfield, Connecticut. Robin Young.

About the Author

Janet Spurr has been visiting
the beach all her life. Between the
sand and the waves she has found paradise. And much more which she brings to
you in the pages of Beach Chair Diaries. When
not at the beach she works as a sales rep for women's
accessory lines, which she sells to the six New England
states. This brings her to the shores of Maine, Lake
Champlain, Vermont, the lakes of New Hampshire,
Rhode Island's beaches, Cape Cod and of course, the
North Shore of Boston. Although the waters of New
England are home, paradise is in the warm waves of Maui
as well as the other Hawaiian islands. Someday, she hopes
to spread the Aloha Spirit throughout New England.

She is a member of the National Writers Union, PMA,
Travel Publishers Association, IPNE, Independent
Publishers of New England, Marblehead Chamber of
Commerce, Dolphin Yacht Club, Colby-Sawyer College
Class correspondent and Trinity Church in Boston.

She hopes to write many more books and visit many
more beaches.

To send your friends Beach Chair Diaries

Please fax this order form to: 781-639-7725

Or go to: www.janetspurr.com

Name: _____

Address: _____

City: _____

State: _____ Zip Code: _____

Telephone: _____

Email Address: _____

Each Copy: $14.95

Shipping: $3.25

CPSIA information can be obtained at www.ICGtesting.com
Printed in the USA
266248BV00001B/6/P